CW00662211

Rock Junket
New York City

The Ultimate Source to New York City's
Rock n' Roll Landmarks

Researched and Written by Bobby Pinn

First Edition 2009

First published by Dog Ear Publishing
4010 W. 86th Street, Ste H
Indianapolis, IN 46268
www.dogearpublishing.net

ISBN: 978-160844-222-5

This paper is acid free and meets all ANSI standards for archival quality paper.
Printed in the United States of America

"Music fans are the life support for rock history."

—Pinn

My name is Ron Colinear, a.k.a. *Bobby Pinn*.

People always ask me why Bobby Pinn? I chose the name
Bobby Pinn because most of my rock idols had cool names
that weren't their birth names. Iggy, Joey Ramone, Johnny
Thunders, Sid Vicious and Richard Hell. The "Pinn" of course
came from the punk scene that Richard Hell helped create with
his well-worn T-shirts held together by safety pins. Also Sid and
the Germs played a part. The name changes worked well for
my rock idols and it seems to have worked well on my end, as
nowadays my friends and customers call me Pinn.

> My story starts in the spring of 2001. I started a rock
> n' roll walking tour of the East Village in New York
> City and named it Rock Junket. The business started
> out as a hobby to keep me busy on weekends and
> keep my mind off my music-industry job that was
> consuming too much of my time and bumming me
> out. I spent over 17 years in the music business
> and worked with many of my favorite bands,
> including Rancid, Nirvana, the Ramones, Smashing
> Pumpkins and B.B. King. I set up the very last
> Ramones in-store at Tower Records in the East
> Village in the fall of 1998. The music business was
> fun and I met some very cool people (and plenty of
> assholes), but I have no regrets. I found the industry
> fun, exciting and challenging, but between 1998 and
> 2003 it wasn't any of that. It became a struggle to

make it through each day. It was run by a bunch of squares that were more interested in their Range Rovers, expense accounts and lavish lifestyles than the welfare of the artists. I witnessed bands signing away their life on the dotted line. I felt bad for the musicians that would need to endure this agony. So I began looking for a back-up plan that still involved music and New York City, thus giving birth to Rock Junket.

I love New York City, and without a doubt it's my favorite city in the world. The creativity, the adrenaline, the arts, music and food is unparalleled. The slogan "I Love NY" is known worldwide. It was a phrase created in 1977 by Milton Glaser to help promote tourism in New York. The city needed to boost tourism because 1977 was a low point for New York City, what with a blackout, a serial killer and a financial crisis lowering its boom on the city. As an early teen I remember customizing, with a black Sharpie, my white Hanes T-shirts with bands and slogans like "Ramones," "New York City Rocks" and "New York Dolls." My mom and dad never understood why I would "destroy" three perfectly good T-shirts, but they saw my passion for music and New York and let me have my way.

I'm a huge fan of the New York rock scene of the '60s and '70s. Some of my favorite artists and bands are the Ramones, New York Dolls, the Velvet Underground, the Dictators, Television, the Heartbreakers, Blondie, Patti Smith, Johnny Thunders, Richard Hell and many others that were associated with New York City. I loved reading about the scene that unfolded at CBGB, Max's Kansas City, the Mudd Club, the Palladium, Andy Warhol's Factory, the Electric Circus and the Fillmore East. I looked forward to getting my copies of *Rolling Stone*, *Crawdaddy*, *Creem*, *PUNK*, *Circus* and *The Village Voice* (which I had to buy from a porno newsstand on Route 22 in Monroeville—six miles from my parents' house), and reading articles about the rock scene from such great writers as Lester Bangs, Greil Marcus, Cameron Crowe, Ben Fong-Torres, Robert Christgau and Hunter S. Thomson's political slant. As a teenager growing up in Pittsburgh, I always thought how cool it must have been to have seen the Ramones play CBGB during their early years, going to Warhol's Exploding Plastic Inevitable parties in 1966 featuring the Velvet Underground or being at Max's and seeing Iggy Pop make rock n' roll history. I remember thinking years later that if the New York City punk scene never happened, some rock n' roll demon from beyond would have created it and placed it in New York City anyway.

So my passion for music and New York City paved the way for my Rock Junket walking tours. I love talking about the music from those eras, and I get to meet cool people from all over the world that take my tours. But my passion and hunger for discovering more about New York City music history led me to do more and more research. Within a couple of years I had boxes of articles, magazines, books, CDs and videos. Then I started taking pictures of sites and concerts in the city, and then the obsession really kicked in. I began compiling information that I thought would be a great addition to my walking tours and would

make any music lover's visit to New York a memorable one. I had so much information about the bands and different sites, and what I learned was so cool and obscure, that I knew the information would make a great rock n' roll advisor.

So what you're holding now is a few years of research and fact checking and conversations I've had with locals, burnouts, hipsters, punks and scenesters. Although many of the people I spoke with had a fuzzy recollection of the '60s, I do believe if you remember too much from that era you really weren't experiencing it like you should have.

Is this book complete? NO. But neither is New York City. It's constantly changing and evolving much like this source book (and my future). Did I include every club and band in New York City? NO, because many of the clubs and newer bands are not relevant to a historical time like the '60s or '70s. And I didn't include current private residences, as this is not a map of the stars. While this book focuses mainly on rock n' roll, I also included selected sites including the Beat Generation, jazz clubs, the blues, hip-hop and the art world that helped make New York special and unique.

So after years of research in an overflowing one-bedroom Manhattan apartment, I hope you can feel the passion and enjoy the fruits of my labor.

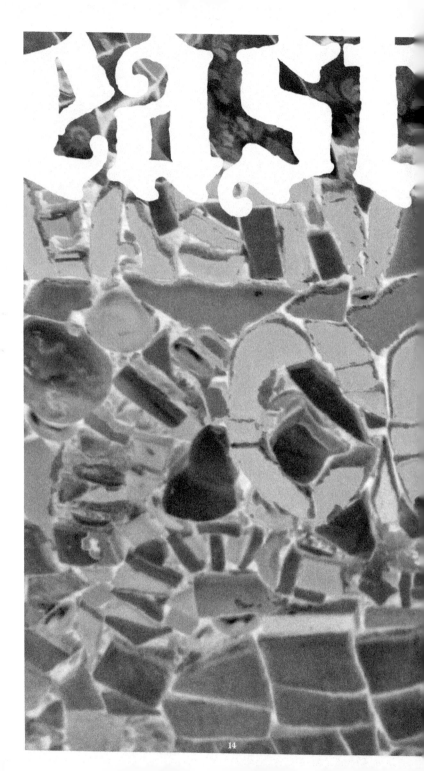

illage

The East Village has often been called the counterculture capital of the world.

The East Village was known as the Lower East Side until the mid-'50s. At that time, city planners and real estate agents were hoping to revitalize the neighborhood, and they decided to remove an above ground train called The El, which ran down 3rd Avenue. Once this was completed in 1955, they renamed the neighborhood the East Village to disassociate it from the slums of the Lower East Side. Soon many of the Beats, musicians and artists moved from the West Village, thus becoming pioneers of a renamed neighborhood.

The East Village was considered a very unhip neighborhood in the early '60s. Andy Warhol once referred to it as "Babbushkaville" due to the very large Polish, Ukrainian and Jewish populations. However in the mid-to-late-'60s things began to change, as Warhol showcased the Velvet Underground at the Dom on St. Marks Place. Although an art, music and underground scene was happening in the East Village, it was Warhol's Exploding Plastic Inevitable parties featuring the Velvet Underground that turned the East Village into a neighborhood that would rival the West Village for clubs, art and music. Shortly after Warhol's Exploding parties, Bill Graham's Fillmore East opened in 1968 and CBGB opened in 1973.

The East Village was on its way as ground zero for the cool, hip and creative in New York City.

Atomic Number 76 rippin' it up at Continental

Trash and Vaudeville, 2008

JOEY RAMONE
Apartment, The St. Mark
115 East 9th Street

This is the Manhattan apartment building that Joey Ramone lived in for more than two decades. Born Jeff Hyman, he changed his name to Joey Ramone when he was 23 years old. Joey lived on the 10th floor. When asked to comment on being in the Ramones he said, "Our years in the business managed to take a lot of fun out of things. It's still fun playing, but they made us miserable. Maybe it was naïve of us to think it was gonna be easier than this. Nobody did anything for us. We got treated like shit." No one ever showed more support for the local New York City music scene than Joey Ramone. Joey passed away at 2:40 pm on Easter Sunday, April 15, 2001. He is laid to rest at Hillside Cemetery in Lyndhurst, New Jersey.

CONTINENTAL
25 3rd Avenue @ St. Marks Place

A landmark club that stopped hosting live music in November 2006, the Continental is located at the corner of St. Marks and 3rd Avenue in the East Village. Prior to being named the Continental, it had an interesting past. In the mid-'70s, this location was the site of Freda's Disco, and it later became a blues and barbecue joint called Jack the Ribber. It then changed owners and became the Continental Divide, which introduced punk, rock and sometimes jazz on the weekends, in addition to serving a killer Vietnamese egg roll. On Halloween of 1991, the newly formed Continental hosted its first show, starring Sea Monster. The Continental's capacity is about 175 people. Some great bands played this small venue in the early and mid-'90s, including the Ramones,

Green Day, Guns N' Roses, the Dictators, Patti Smith, L.E.S. Stitches, Murphy's Law, the Germs, L.A. Guns, the Exploited, Bouncing Souls, D Generation, the Addicts and the Wallflowers.

On January 13, 1993, Iggy Pop played a gig at the club, only to have the New York City Fire and Police Departments show up, putting an early end to the concert as a result of an overcrowded situation. On December 11, 2000, Joey Ramone performed at the Continental for his last show ever. Today the club features an extensive happy hour with cheap drinks, some TV screens and a good jukebox.

ST. MARKS HOTEL
2 St. Marks Place

This was the former site of the Valencia Hotel, a rundown flophouse-style hotel on the outskirts of the Bowery. The Sagamore Cafeteria was located on the ground floor of this building in the '50s and '60s, and was frequented by Beat writers during that time. Jack Kerouac once referred to the Sagamore as the cafeteria for "respectable bums." In the late '50s, a legendary jazz club called the Five Spot occupied the ground floor facing Cooper Square. James Leo Herlihy featured the hotel in the 1971 novel *Season of the Witch*.

The New York punk scene also had its share of memories here. Many musicians, writers and artists have crashed at the hotel over the years, including Dee Dee Ramone and Johnny Thunders. Alan K, of the band Road Vultures, met his untimely death at the hotel in 1996. Self-described "Public Animal Number 1" and New York punk rock vocalist of the Murder Junkies, GG Allin (real name Kevin Michael Allin), lived here during the early '90s. It was at the St. Marks Hotel that portions of the documentary *Hated* were filmed. Some interesting clips in that documentary include a scene from the Geraldo Rivera Show where GG is asked why he urinates and throws his own feces at his fans during live shows. GG said, "My body is a rock n' roll temple, and therefore my body fluids are communion to my fans." Touché!

TRASH AND VAUDEVILLE
4 St. Marks Place

This building is a 19th-century townhouse and former site of the Bridge Theater. The Bridge Theater was an improvisational theater in the East Village. During a 1967 improv performance, actors burned the American flag, thus resulting in the theater closing temporarily. Yoko Ono was one of the many artists that held "happenings" here in the late '60s, staging multimedia-type events. Yoko showcased art, music, fashion and film. It became Trash and Vaudeville in 1975 and has been a staple of St. Marks Place ever since. Plenty of rockers have shopped here including Joan Jett, Keith Richards, Iggy Pop, Dee Dee Ramone, Debbie Harry and Joey Ramone. Lots of punk, rock and goth wear and a super cool staff make Trash a must visit for all your rock clothing. When visiting, give a shout-out to rocker extraordinaire Jimmy Webb!

KIM'S VIDEO
6 St. Marks Place

Kim's video is a small New York City CD and video chain. This location was well stocked with obscure import discs and films. I'm sure you would have found something that you wouldn't find anywhere else. They stocked plenty of CDs DVDs books and vinyl. The store was easy to find—it was a big bright-yellow building on St. Marks Place between 2nd and 3rd Avenues. This location was also the former site of St. Marks Baths, a popular gay bathhouse that closed in 1985. Unfortunately, this location of Kim's closed in January of 2009.

Kim's Video, 2008

IAN'S
5 St. Marks Place

Ian's has been around for a long time on St. Marks, and used to bill itself as "the original stage and evening wear boutique since 1972." Inspired by the New York Dolls' music and fashion, Ian was inspired to open a hip clothing boutique in the Village. Ian's was the first New York retailer to import the fashions of Vivienne Westwood and Malcolm McClaren from their Sex Store in London, introducing bondage pants and shirts to the Big Apple. Although the safety-pin shirts were the creation of Richard Hell, it was

Vivienne and Malcolm who seemed to popularize it. an's closed its St. Marks doors in December of 2007.

RELIGIOUS SEX
7 St. Marks Place

This is the former site of Religious Sex clothing store. They used to cater to goth, punk and local clothing labels. It was a great place to shop for cool hip clothing, role-play and cross-dressers, or just to find something hot and sexy for your dominant or submissive side. Some notables that have laid down a credit card here include Prince, Jenny McCarthy, Lisa Marie Presley, Slash, Joan Jett and Alice Cooper. The high rents and gentrification of the East Village forced Religious Sex to close in January of 2004.

Religious Sex, 2003

LENNY BRUCE
Apartment, 13 St. Marks Place

Lenny Bruce was an original, an innovator and a true comedic genius. This apartment was his last New York City residence. Bruce had an edgy comedy routine that is still imitated in some form or another. But as times changed, the routines of many new comedians such as Richard Pryor, Eddie Murphy, Howard Stern, Andrew Dice Clay and Chris Rock became even more outrageous. But during Lenny's era this material was viewed as shocking and unheard of, which is why he was an original. Lenny Bruce moved to the East Village in 1964. He died from a drug overdose in the bath-

room of his Hollywood Hills home on August 3, 1966.

CONEY ISLAND HIGH
15 St. Marks Place

Coney Island High was a rock club started by New York City band D Generation in the 90s. The club was part of a thriving rock scene in the East Village in the mid-to late '90s, playing host to the Green Door Party, (an idea that began in a Chelsea loft in 1988). The Green Door crowd was cool and diversified, and they partied to tunes by Iggy, the New York Dolls, T. Rex, Slade, the Stones, the Ramones and Grand Funk, spun by guest DJs like Jayne County and Jesse Malin.

Coney Island High certainly had a great location for a rock club. Down the street

The Dom 40 years after Warhol's parties

was a drug and rehab center, nearby was the notorious St. Marks Hotel and New York University, with its teeming party-student population. It was a frequent hangout for musicians, including Joey Ramone, Joe Strummer, Iggy Pop, Debbie Harry and touring and local artists and musicians. Coney Island High closed in late 1999, due in part to a rent increase, and then Mayor Rudolph Giuliani's "Quality of Life Law." The law stated that no more live music venues would be a part of St. Marks Place from 3rd Avenue to Tompkins Square Park. The law remains in effect to this day, but there are a few "weekend brunch" spots that offer jazz. That is fucking weak.

THE DOM
19–25 St. Marks Place

This is the former site of the Polski Dom Narodowy National Dance Hall. In April of 1966, Andy Warhol's Exploding Plastic Inevitable music and light show debuted at the Polski Dom. During this time Warhol was managing the Velvet Underground, and it was his wish to showcase their talent, so they became Warhol's house band. Warhol also planned on showing his voyeuristic movies, such as *Sleep*, a five-hour movie starring John Giorno sleeping on a couch, *Empire*, an eight-hour movie of daylight moving across the Empire State Building, *Eat* starring pop art's Robert Indiana, and *Blowjob*, which didn't suck. All the walls in the Dom were painted white so Warhol could better screen his movies. The Velvet Underground and the movies would play at the same time. Admission to the event was $2.00–$2.50, depending on the night. Warhol also hired dancers to carry props through the crowd, such as eight-foot plastic hypodermic needles, bull whips and large crosses. After one month his lease was up, so Warhol took the Exploding party to five other cities throughout the U.S., including Chicago, Cincinnati and San Francisco. He returned to the Dom, which was under new management, and changed the name of the party to The Balloon Farm.

However, in 1967, the lease changed hands again and was transferred to

Gem Spa, 2008

a former William Morris agent named Jerry Brandt. Jerry created the Electric Circus, and often showcased talent from the William Morris Agency. They hired magicians, trapeze artists, palm readers and other carnival-like performers to entertain the crowd. The light show was incredible, often referred to as a "hallucinogenic light bath." They painted the front of the building blue which remained the main color until 2001. As the parties moved forward, the Electric Circus became the place to go in the East Village to party, hear music and see light shows. Other musicians besides the Velvet Underground who played at the Electric Circus include Santana, Jimi Hendrix, the Chambers Brothers and the Grateful Dead. In between music sets, flame throwing jugglers and trapeze artists would entertain the crowd.

The Electric Circus suffered a major setback in March of 1970 when a timed bomb went off, injuring 17 people. The bomb also destroyed a portion of the stage, blasted a hole in the wall and covered the club in white ash. Attendance dropped from 3,000 a week to 300 a week. To this day the NYPD has no idea who set the bomb, but they speculate the culprit was someone who was upset with the cost of the $4.00 admission.

The Electric Circus era came to an end during the summer of 1971. New clubs tried their hand at that space after the Electric Circus but it never worked out. Ironically it became a drug and rehab center for nearly two decades, complete with all of the original Warhol fixtures, like mirrored ceilings and disco balls. Must have been quite a flashback to get clean where you blew your mind years earlier! The Polski Dom was converted to residential apartments in 2003 as the neighborhood continued its gentrification.

ABBIE HOFFMAN
Apartment, 30 St. Marks Place

Abbie Hoffman was a well-known political activist. During the years 1967–1968, Hoffman and his wife Anita lived here in a fourth-floor apartment, for which they paid $101 a month. This is where Abbie, Jerry Rubin and their friends laid the

Fillmore East, 2008

couple of racks of clothing from their own wardrobe, and then went on to create the world's first alternative cosmetic and hair-color line called Manic Panic. Its vibrant colors and punky chic made it an instant hit with rockers in New York City and elsewhere. The line is sold worldwide now and remains very popular. Over the years, fans of Manic Panic hair color have included Cyndi Lauper, Joss Stone, Davey Havok of A.F.I., Kate Pierson of the B-52s and New York's very own Lunachicks.

KHYBER PASS
34 St. Marks Place

Groove was in the heart for the New York band Deee-Lite, who used to live in this building on St. Marks Place. Deee-Lite were a trippy New York City pop band that flirted with drag culture and enjoyed their greatest success in the early '90s with their single "Groove is in the Heart."

CLUB 57
57 St. Marks Place

Located in the basement of a church, this club was managed by Ann Magnuson. It became a hangout for musicians and artists in the '70s and '80s. It was described as having a "Punk Do-It-Yourself Aesthetic," which inspired such cool theme nights as "Putt Putt Reggae" and "Model World of Glue Night." The first gig that Sonic Youth played under that name was here on May 8, 1981. Keith Haring, Debi Mazar and Kenny Scharf also hung here.

GEM SPA
131 2nd Avenue @ St. Marks Place

Allen Ginsberg once referred to the Gem Spa as "an oasis in the middle of a jungle," because it was the one thing on St.

groundwork for the Yippie Movement (Youth International Party). He often said that he would look out his window and watch the counter culture of the world evolve on St. Marks Place.

MANIC PANIC
33 St. Marks Place

In 1977, the Bellomo sisters, Tish and Snooky, who were also in the original lineup for Blondie, took the fashion world for a spin. They opened America's first punk-rock boutique on St. Marks Place. During that time, St. Marks Place was not the bustling street it is today. It was quite rundown, with many empty storefronts. However, they found a spot at 33 St. Marks Place for $250 a month to open their own business. They started with a few go-go boots and a

Marks Place that never really seemed to change. It was open seven days a week, 24 hours a day, even during those lean-and-mean times of the '70s. It still remains a 24/7 spot. The New York Dolls posed in front of the Gem Spa for the back cover of their first album. Legendary rock photographer Roberta Bayley took the shot. Photographer Toshi shot the front cover for a reported $900. Mercury Records, the label that signed the Dolls, initially wanted the band to pose as mannequins in an antique store, but they refused. The Dolls routinely used the Gem Spa as a backdrop for show flyers and promotional posters. The Gem Spa also claims to have perfected the New York City egg cream, which is seltzer water, a splash of very cold almost-crystallized milk and chocolate syrup. Many people consider Gem Spa a New York City landmark, so stop by, get an egg cream and sing "Personality Crisis!"

FILLMORE EAST
105 2nd Avenue @ 6th Street

In the early 1900s, this was the Loews Commodore movie theater, a very large theater that held nearly 2,700 people. It went through many transitions and name changes over the years. The space turned into a silent movie theater, a Yiddish theater, was known as the Village Theater and then the Second Avenue Theater, before it became the legendary Fillmore East in April of 1968.

The Fillmore's founder, Bill Graham, was also a very clever rock promoter with innovative ideas that I sometimes wish were imitated today. The Fillmore always had early and late shows at 8:00 pm and midnight. Three bands would normally perform—two openers and a headliner. Graham enjoyed mixing up the genres of the three bands, sometimes pairing gospel with hard rock. Bill Graham said that he wanted to open people's ears to all types of music.

The first gig was on March 8, 1968, and featured Janis Joplin headlining, with opening bands Albert King and Tim Buckley. Albert King's drummer went AWOL from the U.S. military to perform at this gig. Needless to say the MPs found out and physically removed him from his drum kit during the second show. Led Zeppelin performed at the Fillmore East for the first time in January of 1969. It was the last date on their first U.S. tour. It's kind of hard to imagine today, but Led Zeppelin was the opening band and Iron Butterfly was the headliner. The New York City audience was so turned on by Led Zep that they called them back for numerous encores, a big no-no for opening bands. They were greeted backstage by Iron Butterfly's manager, who refused to let his band go on, citing they were upstaged by this new band called Led Zeppelin.

Many of our favorite bands performed at the Fillmore East, including the Doors,

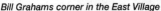

Bill Grahams corner in the East Village

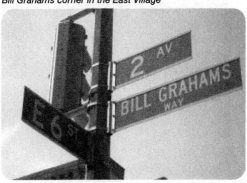

the Beach Boys, Neil Young, Jimi Hendrix, Grateful Dead, the Animals, Frank Zappa and many others. The Who debuted their rock opera *Tommy* here in October of 1969 with King Crimson opening. Check your CD collection, because I'm sure you have one of the many great albums recorded here, including *The Allman Brothers at Fillmore East*, *Band of Gypsys* by Jimi Hendrix, *Humble Pie's Performance: Rockin the Fillmore*, *Frank Zappa and The Mothers of Invention Fillmore East: June 1971*, *Miles Davis at Fillmore* and most recently, *Neil Young and Crazy Horse Live at the Fillmore East*.

It all came to an end on June 27, 1971, when the Fillmore East closed its doors for good. Reasons Graham cited were higher pay for artists, rising ticket prices and his desire to work with Martin Scorsese on the film *The Last Waltz*, featuring The Band. The last night at the Fillmore East featured Mountain, Edgar Winter, Rick Derringer, Country Joe and the Fish, the Beach Boys, Albert King, J Geils Band, and the Allman Brothers Band.

After the close of the Fillmore East, the space became a gay dance club called the Saint, and it's now a branch of Emigrant Bank. The bank has recognized the history of the building and adorned its walls with classic posters and pictures of the bands that played there.

Bill Graham, born Wolfgang Grajonca in Berlin, Germany, died in a helicopter accident in October of 1991 at the age of 60. The corner of East 6th Street and 2nd Avenue is named *Bill Graham's Way*.

RATNER'S
111 2nd Avenue

Ratner's kosher dairy restaurant was opened in 1905 and was a favorite of the Fillmore East crowd. It was open 24 hours a day, seven days a week. Bill Graham referred to Ratner's as his unofficial office. He brought everyone here for the blintzes, including John Lennon, Jimi Hendrix, Jerry Garcia, Janis Joplin and Grace Slick. The deli relocated to 138 Delancey Street, and the building faced demolition in 2004. During the final pre-demolition closing event, held on December 14, 2004, the prices were rolled back to those of 1905.

Holiday Cocktail Lounge, 2007

ST. MARKS BAR AND GRILL
132 1st Avenue @ St. Marks Place

The St. Marks Bar and Grill was a very small but cool neighborhood bar located on St. Marks Place at 1st Avenue in the East Village. In 1981, the Rolling Stones released their critically acclaimed album *Tattoo You*. The Stones released numerous singles from the album and shot five videos. One of those was "Waiting on a Friend," which was filmed at the St. Marks Bar and Grill. In the video, Mick Jagger is waiting on a set of stairs (at the *Physical Graffiti* building) with a few Rastafarians—including Peter Tosh, waiting for his "friend" Keith Richards. They meet and make the short walk to the St. Marks Bar and Grill, where Charlie Watts, Ron Wood and Bill Wyman greet them inside. The outside of the bar was covered with *Tattoo You* album covers and other Stones images. After the video shoot was completed, the Stones picked up their guitars and played a few songs for the staff and video crew. Among those songs was Jimmy Reed's "You Don't Have to Go." Capacity of the St. Marks Bar and Grill was about 75 people, so seeing the Stones jam in that tiny bar must have been cool as shit.

JOAN MITCHELL
Art Studio
60 St. Marks Place

A celebrated expressionist painter who was influenced by Willem de Kooning, Joan Mitchell made huge inroads in the New York art scene in the '50s. This was the site of her studio from 1951 until she moved to France in 1955. Joan was one of just a few female painters who achieved critical acclaim during the 50s. She was born in Chicago on February 12, 1925, and passed away in France on October 30, 1992.

HOLIDAY COCKTAIL LOUNGE
75 St. Marks Place

I love a great East Village dive bar, and this one is located right on St. Marks Place. It's got a cool neighborhood vibe with a small bar upfront and some tables and booths in the back. They serve all walks of life too. When Madonna first moved to New York City and lived on East 4th Street, it was rumored that the Holiday was the inspiration for her number one dance-club hit, "Holiday." I don't know about that. How about getting a drink at the bar and listening to the song—then decide if the rumor is correct? Also, on their 1997 self-titled release, the Bouncing Souls wrote a song about the bar called "Holiday Cocktail Lounge." Bottoms Up!

LED ZEPPELIN
Physical Graffiti Building
96–98 St. Marks Place

Plenty of album covers were shot in New York City, but probably none more famous then Led Zeppelin's cover for their double album *Physical Graffiti*. The album cover features a die-cut picture of a New York City tenement building and features many celebrities and illustrations in the windows, including Neil Armstrong, Elizabeth Taylor, King Kong and Charles Atlas.

Graphic design artist Peter Corriston, who later went on to design the *Some Girls* and *Tattoo You* album covers for the Rolling Stones, designed *Physical Graffiti*. The album was intended to be the first release on Led Zeppelin's new Swan Song record label. Because of the intricate die-cut design, *Physical Graffiti* was delayed, and Bad Company's debut album was the first LP released on Swan

Song. The steps of this building were also used in the Rolling Stones video, "Waiting on a Friend," in 1981. Was it a coincidence that Peter Corriston designed *Tattoo You*, and the *Physical Graffiti* steps were used in that Stones video?

SIN-E
124 St. Marks Place

Pronounced Shih-Nay, this small coffee shop/performance space opened in 1989. There were some great music performances here, including those by Sinead O'Connor and Shane McGowan. One night, Bono from U2 stopped by and played piano. In 1993, Jeff Buckley recorded an EP here called *Live at Sin-e*. High rent was one of the reasons Sin-e moved to its second location at North 8th Street in Brooklyn. Sin-e then found its final location back in Manhattan, at Attorney Street near Stanton, on the Lower East Side.

TOMPKINS SQUARE PARK
Avenue A—10th Street to 7th Street

New York City has some beautiful public and private parks, and each has a very rich history. Tompkins Square Park is a 17-acre park located in Alphabet City in the East Village. The city named the park after Daniel Tompkins, who was a governor of New York in the early 1800s, and who abolished slavery in the state of New York. Daniel Tompkins also became Vice President of the United States under President John Monroe.

In 1966, a bandshell was erected. Performers who played there included Jimi Hendrix, the Grateful Dead, Santana and the Fugs.

Tompkins Square Park has also gained a reputation as a center for demonstrations and protests throughout the years. It also became the center of attention when the residents of the East Village

Joe Strummer mural in Alphabet City, 2007

and Lower East Side rallied against gentrification of the neighborhood. In the late '80s it became known as "Tent City," because of the homeless who slept on benches, in boxes and in makeshift tents. During that time, the city felt that they lost control of the park and wanted to reshape and upgrade the neighborhood. The New York City Fire and Police departments were called in to evacuate and help relocate the homeless. Riots occurred and soon thereafter gentrification of the neighborhood. The city regained control of the park and decided to remodel it by adding handball courts, a swimming pool, a dog run and lots of open space.

Led Zeppelin Physical Graffiti

The bandshell was eventually torn down. The East Village and Tompkins Square Park are also the home of the *Howl Festival*, a three-day summer-ending event spotlighting the arts and creativity of the East Village. On the third day of the weekend festival is the *Charlie Parker Jazz Fest*, a daylong celebration of jazz and entertainment.

JOE STRUMMER
Mural/Niagara Bar
112 Avenue A @ 7th Street

Niagara Bar is located in Alphabet City (Avenues A through D), and is partially owned by ex-D Generation musician Jesse Malin. If you're a fan of the Clash, you'll definitely want to stop by and have a drink. On November 16, 2003, the Niagara Bar was the centerpiece of

a video for Joe Strummer's cover of Bob Marley's "Redemption Song." The video shows a graffiti artist painting a portrait of Strummer on the outside of the bar, mixed with footage of Strummer and his band, the Mescaleros, in concert. The video features cameos from a few of Joe's friends, including Rancid, Matt Dillon, Jesse Malin and Jim Jarmusch. The portrait remains today and is a memorable New York City tribute to a great man, musician and very influential band.

PYRAMID CLUB
101 Avenue A

The Pyramid Club, opened in 1979, is another East Village landmark and one of the first clubs to welcome and embrace the gay scene.

CMJ is an annual weeklong music festival, hosted by New York City and the

College Music Journal tip sheet, that showcases new bands and features an abundance of panels related to the music business. Nirvana played their very first New York City show here during the CMJ festival on July 18, 1989.

The Red Hot Chili Peppers also played their first-ever gig in New York here. In 1985, a group of regulars at the club created Wigstock, a one-day-long drag festival that was held in nearby Tompkins Square Park, but later moved to Chelsea Piers on the West Side to accommodate the large crowds. The festival ran for nearly 13 years. Madonna also held an AIDS benefit here.

NICO/PYRAMID CLUB
Apartment, 101 Avenue A, 2nd floor

Nico was one of the most fascinating and beautiful women of the '60s. She

The "Bird House" Charlie Parker's former home

was born Christa Paffgen in Cologne Germany, on October 16, 1938. A model, she became part of the Velvet Underground in 1966 and toured with them for a year. It was at this location that Nico used to rent a loft on the second floor, shortly after her arrival in New York City. Nico died of a brain hemorrhage while riding her bicycle on July 18, 1988, on the island of Ibiza.

EAST VILLAGE OTHER
147 Avenue A

The *East Village Other*, first published in 1965, was one of the first counterculture magazines published in the U.S. The look of the magazine was cool, funky and psychedelic. They ceased operation in 1973.

ODESSA DINER
119 Avenue A

The Odessa Diner, opposite Tompkins Square Park, is a 24-hour diner, and a favorite of musicians, artists and locals. It was reported that after joining Black Flag on stage to sing "Clocked In" at nearby bar 7A, Henry Rollins met the band at Odessa a few days later to discuss joining.

PSYCHEDELICATESSEN
164 Avenue A

Designer Betsy Johnson opened perhaps the coolest hippie headshop in New York City for a couple of years between 1966–1968. The building went through a redesign that merged 162 with 164 Avenue A.

BROWNIES
169 Avenue A

Brownies opened in 1989 and was at one time considered the

Manitoba's rockin' Avenue B since January 1999

premier showcase for hot upcoming bands in the East Village. Ben Folds Five, Creed, the Verve Pipe, Veruca Salt and many others made their New York City debut at this club. In 1998, it became Hi-Fi after one of the owners took a shot at the corporate world and then decided it wasn't for him. It's the home of EL DJ or Extra Large Digital Jukebox. It is billed as the biggest jukebox in the world with over 32,000 songs and more than 3,000 CDs. The bar does not host live music today, but it certainly is a cool spot to drop by and get a drink.

SAVE THE ROBOTS
Avenue B
between 2nd and 3rd Street

This was an after-hours punk-rock establishment in Alphabet City, located near Tompkins Square Park. The club operated from the early '80s to the late '90s, and the basement dance floor was always packed and quite loud. Many of the customers were the squatters and the homeless from Tompkins Square Park, who slept during the day in the park, then spent all night at Save

the Robots. After it closed, it later reopened as a club called Guernica.

GG ALLIN
Death Site, 29 Avenue B

After performing a portion of a live concert at the outdoor venue the Gas Station, GG Allin, singer of the Murder Junkies, overdosed on heroin in this apartment. The unfortunate locale was owned by Johnny Puke, (a.k.a. John Handley Hurt) and Johnny's girlfriend, Dwanna Younts. GG Allin died the morning of June 28, 1993.

EAST VILLAGE EYE
43 Avenue B

The *East Village Eye* was a monthly tabloid that focused on the East Village music, art and fashion scenes. Founded by Leonard Abrams, it was an edgy form of pop culture.

MANITOBA'S
99 Avenue B

This was the former site of the Avenue B Social Club, and now the site of Manitoba's. Owned and operated by Dictators' lead singer, Handsome Dick Manitoba, this cool punk-rock bar displays many photos on its walls including images of the Ramones, the New York Dolls, Sex Pistols, the Rolling Stones, the Dictators, Television, Blondie, the Damned, Iggy and many more. Some of the photographers featured are Bob Gruen, Mick Rock, Godlis and Roberta Bayley. At a time when iPods have become the norm for bar music, Manitoba's still sports one of the best jukeboxes in the city. Stop by, get a beer and pick up a Dictators T-shirt!

CHARLIE PARKER
Apartment
151 Avenue B @ 10th Street

Often called "The Birdhouse," alto-sax jazz great Charlie Parker lived here from 1950–1954. The building is an 1849 Gothic style row house that he shared with Chan Richard son and their children during the height of his career. During the time Bird lived here, the neighbor-

hood was not the vibrant trendy area that it is today. There were gutted buildings, no retail stores and lots of drug trafficking.

The city of New York recognized Charlie Parker's greatness and contributions to jazz and, during the '90s, made his former home a national landmark. The city also renamed Avenue B between 7th and 10th Streets *Charlie Parker Place*. Tompkins Square Park is the site of the annual *Howl Festival,* which is a three-day event addressing the artists, music and creativity of the East Village. The third day of the festival is the *Charlie Parker Jazz Fest*, which features great jazz musicians performing all day long.

IGGY POP
Apartment, Christodora House
143 Avenue B @ 9th Street

Even though Iggy is a native of Ann Arbor/Detroit, we think of him as an adopted New Yorker. The Stooges recorded

Iggy's Avenue B apartment building

their debut album at the Hit Factory in 1969, and Iggy named a solo record *Avenue B* after the street he lived on in Alphabet City. Iggy lived at the Christodora House for the better part of the '90s. His album *Avenue B* featured a jazz trio from New York City called Modeski, Martin and Wood. It has a bit of a different feel than most Iggy solo records, but I thought it was a cool diversion, and I loved the tour that supported it.

The Christodora House was built in 1928 as a settlement house for low-income families and minorities. The real estate and condo boom of the '80s in New York City changed many neighboroods and buildings, and during that time the Christodora House went condo. Ironically, the Christadora House became a symbol of anti-gentrification during the Tompkins Square Park riots in the late '80s. Rioters were throwing objects into the lobby of the Christadora such as plants, garbage and barricades while yelling "yuppie scum!"

GAS STATION
194 East 2nd Street

The former site of a gas station eventually became a music venue called the Gas Station. The venue and stage area reeked of gasoline, and oil, and it was here that GG

Jimi Hendrix East 9th Street apartment

Allin and the Murder Junkies performed their last gig. A few hardcore bands took the stage that steamy hot June afternoon before GG Allin emerged naked from the apartment of his friend Johnny Puke. GG was allegedly fueled on cocaine, alcohol and rage, and a riot occurred after just a few minutes on stage. Police were summoned, and the show ended, as did GG's life, as he overdosed on heroin later that day, June 28, 1993.

C-SQUAT
155 Avenue C

C-Squat served as a squatter's house and venue for many of the punk bands that called it home. Some of the bands that lived and played here include Choking Victim and Morning Glory. In 2002, New York City made it possible for the squatters to develop the building into low-income co-ops.

LEADBELLY
Apartment, 414 East 10th Street

His real name was Huddie Leadbetter, but fans knew him as Leadbelly. He wrote "Where Did You Sleep Last Night," "The Gallows Pole," "Midnight Special" and "Black Betty," among others. Those songs became hits for many rock/punk bands years after his death, including Nirvana, Led Zeppelin, Creedence Clearwater Revival, the White Stripes, the Animals, Tom Waits and Pearl Jam. He was an inspirational and creative musical force who lived in this building during the '40s. Musicians that would drop by to jam or say hello included Woody Guthrie and Pete Seeger. Leadbelly died of Lou Gehrig's Disease in New York City in 1949.

Webster Hall waiting for the gals to roll in

HEROIN ALLEY
East 2nd Street and Avenue C

This street corner in Alphabet City was considered one of the major drug-trafficking areas in the East Village during the '60s and '70s.

SCOTT WEILAND
Drug-Bust Site, 20 Avenue D

Stone Temple Pilots front man Scott Weiland was busted outside the Lillian Ward Public Housing Project on June 1, 1998. Police found ten decks, or $10.00 packs of heroin, on Weiland. During this time Weiland had just released a solo album called *12 Bar Blues*.

MADONNA
First New York City Apartment
234 East 4th Street, 4A

New York is a remarkable city where the rich often live right next to the poor. I always liked discovering where musicians, artists, writers and bands lived before they made it big and moved into their Jersey mansions or Central Park West apartments.

When Madonna first moved to New York City, she had $30.00, a winter coat and one suitcase. She told the cabbie "drop me off in the middle of everything," so he took her to Times Square. It was a few days before Madonna found her first apartment. She chose Alphabet City in the East Village, or perhaps it chose her, because of the cheap rents at the time. In the late '70s, this neighborhood was full of drugs, poverty, gangs, squatters, homeless, low-income housing units and cheap apartments. Certainly not like it is today. A remarkable story because within a few years her debut release would go five times platinum in the U.S. alone, and she was beginning to change pop culture forever.

JIMI HENDRIX
East Village Apartment
321 East 9th Street

Jimi Hendrix lived here during 1969, which made it easy for Jimi to get to the Fillmore East on 2nd Avenue. It was during this time that Hendrix recorded his legendary New Year's Eve show at the Fillmore. The year 1969 was also a time when Hendrix did a lot of jamming with Steven Stills, Johnny Winter, Billy Cox and Sharon Layne at the Record Plant, and at Steve Paul's The Scene in Midtown Manhattan. In August of 1969 Jimi traveled upstate to Bethel, New York to close out the famed *Woodstock Music and Art Fair*.

WEBSTER HALL
125 East 11th Street

Once you step inside Webster Hall it's hard to believe that it was built in 1886. In the early 1900s this was a very large dance hall, and during the '50s RCA Records converted the building into their recording studio. It became the legendary rock club the Ritz in 1980. Guns N' Roses, Prince, the Dead Boys, the Ramones, Charlie Watts and Eric Clapton all performed on the Ritz stage. After six years, the Ritz relocated and Webster Hall was reborn. You may remember Madonna's infamous *Pajama Party*, which was filmed here for MTV. It's rumored that Al Capone was an owner of Webster Hall in the '20s. During that time it was sometimes referred to as the "Devil's Playground."

Today Webster Hall plays host to many popular rock and punk bands, and they also host some pretty serious dance parties. Capacity is about 600. The club

also operates Webster Hall Records, which has released several successful dance compilations.

TOWER RECORDS
Former Site
East 4th Street and Broadway

This former site of Tower Records occupied a couple of floors of the Silk Building, and was an East Village favorite. Bands or artists that have performed in-stores or had signings here include Madonna, Keith Richards, Iggy Pop, Green Day, Nirvana and the Ramones—who did their last in-store at this location. The New York Dolls did Towers' very last in-store on July 27, 2006. In the audience was Chrissie Hynde of the Pretenders. Quite a few of the apartments above Tower used to be the homes of rock and movie stars, including Keith Richards, Cher, Tom Cruise, Nicole Kidman and Britney Spears—pre-head and beaver shaving.

KEITH HARING POP SHOP
292 Lafayette Street

Inspired by graffiti art, Keith Haring first drew public attention to his artwork with

Ramones in-store Tower Records, 1998

white chalk drawings in New York City's subway system. This was the site of the Keith Haring Pop Shop, which opened in 1986. Keith's purpose for the shop was to make art affordable to everyone, even if it was on a T-shirt. The Pop Shop closed its doors in August of 2005 due to the high increase in rent.

Keith Haring's last art studio was at 676 Broadway, which is now the home of the *Keith Haring Foundation*, which hopes to sustain, expand and protect his ideals. Keith Haring died of AIDS-related complications in 1990 at the age of 31.

PUNK MAGAZINE
225 Lafayette Street

The definitive punk magazine was created in 1976 by cartoonist John Holmstrom, Legs McNeil and Ged Dunn. They published 15 issues from 1976–1979, focused on the New York City punk scene of the mid-to-late-'70s. The original name of the magazine was to be *Teenage News* after an unreleased New York Dolls song, but Legs suggested the name *Punk*. The first cover featured John Holmstrom's cartoon drawing of punk icon Lou Reed. *Punk* never dies—they still publish occasionally.

CLUB 82
82 East 4th Street

Originally a drag club that opened in 1953, Club 82 featured three shows a night, seven days a week, with a $5.00 cover charge. Kit Russell directed the world-famous cast of 35 femme impersonators. It was also a popular destination for many people in the '50s and '60s, including Hollywood stars such as Liz Taylor, Bob Hope, Milton Berle, the Gabor sisters and many others. Allegedly, Errol Flynn pulled out his

huge cock one night and began playing the piano with it. Now that's what you call tickling the ivory!

Club 82 started booking bands around 1972, and Another Pretty Face was the house band in 1973. The New York Dolls became a fixture at the club, first playing there on April 17, 1974, and performing in drag except for Johnny Thunders, who refused to wear a dress. The stage was behind the bar, and during those days two hard-scrapple lesbian bartenders named Tommy and Butch operated it. Many bands played here, including the Dictators, Television, the Heartbreakers, the Stilettos and the Brats. It was considered the epicenter of the glam scene in the early '70s, and was frequented by many rock stars including David Bowie, Mick Jagger and Lou Reed.

THE VILLAGE VOICE
36 Cooper Square

Writer Norman Mailer, Dan Wolf and Ed Fancher founded *The Village Voice* in 1955. Winner of three Pulitzer Prizes, *The Voice* remains the bible of New York City's Downtown scene. Among the many writers who have contributed over the years are Henry Miller, Allen Ginsberg and Ezra Pound. It's an excellent source of keeping in touch with news, fashion, art and music in New York City.

CAT CLUB
76 East 13th Street

This place has had more than nine lives, with past spots called Plaid and a trendy club called Spa. But before both of those clubs, it was called the Cat Club. A hip rock club that ruled New York City in the late '80s and early '90s. Many memorable shows took place here, including one that featured Sonic Youth,

CBGB, 2006

Pussy Galore and Blacksnakes. David Bowie, Duran Duran and Stevie Ray Vaughan also gigged here. The Black Crowes played here during their *Shake Your Money Maker* days, as did the Cult, who surprised the fucked-up crowd by going onstage after a Johnny Thunders performance.

ACADEMY OF MUSIC
2 Irving Place @ 14th Street

The Academy of Music was built in 1854, and then rebuilt in 1866 after a fire destroyed the building. The Academy of Music featured opera, vaudeville and silent movies. Capacity was nearly 1,500. The place was demolished in 1926 to make way for the Con Edison building. It then moved across the street in 1927 and began showing movies. It was later renamed the Palladium.

WILLEM de KOONING
Studio, 88 East 10th Street

Willem de Kooning, born April 24, 1904, was a major force in the abstract expressionist movement and was known for his "Women" paintings. Having been born in the Netherlands, de Kooning

arrived in the United States as a stowaway on a British freighter in 1926 and resided at the Hotel Chelsea. Eventually de Kooning and his wife Elaine moved here after being evicted from their West 22nd Street studio in December of 1946. They both lived and worked here through the mid-'50s. Willem de Kooning died on March 19, 1997.

JOE JACKSON
Apartment, 135 East 13th Street

Jackson came to New York City in the spring of 1982 to begin working on the *Night and Day* album at Blue Rock Studio in Soho. After a couple of months, Joe fell in love with the city and resided here in this 13th Street apartment building.

WILLIAM S. BURROUGHS
Bunker, 222 Bowery

If you're a fan of Burroughs you have undoubtedly heard of the "Bunker." It was here that Burroughs lived from 1975–1981 in a windowless apartment that was a former YMCA locker room. The rent was $400 a month, but in 1981, due to new rent guidelines, the rent dou-

From top left: Joey Ramone Memorial April 2001. Many cocktails were consumed at these tables. The men's room, Me and Hilly Kristal. The owner and founder of CBGB. The bands could score a live recording of their show.

CBGB CBGB
OMFUG   OMFUG
$4.50 RED BEER $ 5.50
      BOTTLED
                ORIGINAL SIN CIDER
                RED STRIPE
                AMSTEL LIGHT
$6.00   SHARP'S (non alcoholic)
STRANGERS $6.00   WATER
ROLLING ROCK   CORONA   SODA 3.00
BUD   SIERRA
BUD LIGHT   HEINEKEN
COORS LIGHT   BECK'S REGULAR
YUENGLING   BASS
               BROOKLYN LAGER

D!
AINS
E
D CORE
RDS
T
D MADE
B's
US!

DON'T
FORGET
YER
POSTCARDS
+
STICKERS
NOW ONLY
$1.10

CBGB
& OMFUG

COUNTRY
BLUE
GRASS
BLUES

OTHER
MUSIC
FOR
UPLIFT
GORMAND

315 BOWERY **JUST**
NY NY 10003 **IN!**
BLACK AND CLEAR
SHOT
GLASSES!
4.95 + TAX

PINT
GLASSES!
7.95 + TAX

CB 313 GALLERY

guitar straps
are
$6.00

GORMAN
gorma
"a greedy
ravenous e
in this case

ALWAYS
REFER TO
THE CBGB
WEBSITE!!
WWW.CBGB.COM
1-866-313-CBGB

SAMUEL
ADAMS

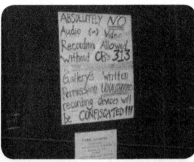

ABSOLUTELY *NO*
Audio (+) Video
Recording Allowed
without CB's 313
Gallery's Written
Permission. *UNAUTHORIZED*
recording devices will
be *CONFISCATED!!!*

From top left: Many objects hung from the ceiling of the club. Beers and prices from 2006. Near the recording area. Sign outside CB's Gallery. So many people asked what CBGB stood for they put up a sign.

We are Closing
October 15th 2006
Yes *all* *3* venues!!!
For More information
go to CBGB.Com!!

"THANK
YOU NYC
&
HOPE TO
BE BACK
SOON"

– HILLY KRISTAL

From top left: The morning after it closed. Urinal inventory day in the Bowery. Artifacts of the club being saved. After Hilly passed away in 2007. The afternoon of the last day.

bled to $800 per month. Burroughs then moved to Lawrence, Kansas, where he remained until his death in 1997 at the age of 83. Those that visited the Bunker include Mick Jagger, Lou Reed, Allen Ginsberg and Andy Warhol.

CBGB OMFUG
315 Bowery @ Bleecker Street

CBGB Is the birthplace of punk rock and the former site of the Bowery dive the Palace Bar, which adjoined the hotel/flophouse the Palace Hotel. Let's start with the question everyone seems to ask first. CBGB stands for Country BlueGrass Blues, and OMFUG stands for Other Music For Uplifting Gormandizers. Hilly Kristal opened CBGB in December of 1973.

The Bowery was a very unstable neighborhood full of derelicts, drunks, thieves and junkies. It was estimated that during the early 1900s, 25,000 bums lived in the Bowery, residing in flophouses, stairwells, doorways and on the street. When CBGB opened in 1973, within a two block radius, there were at least six flophouses housing more than 2,000 men. Usually when criminals were released from jail or patients from the mental institution, they were put up by the city in one of the many flophouses in the Bowery.

Hilly was in his 40s when he opened CB's, with his motorcycle gang-type look. Years earlier he studied classical violin, sang in the chorus at Radio City Music Hall, booked some college tours of folk and jazz groups and managed legendary jazz club the Village Vanguard, all before he decided to open CBGB. Hilly enjoyed country, blues and folk so he thought it would be a great idea if he opened his own club featuring those genres of music. During the first few months that CBGB was open those were the types of bands that graced the stage. Because of the location of the club, many of those music fans stayed away. Fortunately the country/bluegrass thing didn't work out, and as they say the rest is history.

Hilly made it mandatory that bands play original music. CB's sold food early on but decided that a dressing room was more important, so it replaced the kitchen. The Ramones played their very first gig at CBGB on August 16, 1974, however, it was Television who first saw the CBGB awning up and inquired about performing. Hilly agreed, but only if they played original music, thus adhering to his policy. Television began a residency at the club on March 31, 1974. Television then turned on the Ramones then Blondie, and it exploded from there.

The club closed its doors on October 15, 2006, over a rent dispute. Performing that night was Patti Smith who was joined on stage by Flea of the Red Hot Chili Peppers. Richard Lloyd of Television also jumped on stage and played "Marquee Moon." The show opened with "Piss Factory," and Patti paid tribute to the greats who have played there by performing Blondie's "Tide is High," the Dead Boys, "Sonic Reducer" and the Ramones' "Blitzkrieg Bop," "Beat on the Brat," "(Do You Remember) Rock n' Roll Radio," and "Sheena is a Punk Rocker." Near the end of her set she performed "Gloria," then mentioned "CBGB was expiring at the age of 33, the same age as Jesus." The evening ended with Patti reading the names of artists who have since passed away since playing CBGB.

Joey Ramone day, 2003

A few other facts about CBGB:

- Over 33,000 different bands have played at CBGB: the Ramones, Blondie, the Dictators, Johnny Thunders, the Voidoids, Joe Strummer, Babes in Toyland, the Dead Boys, Richard Hell, Joan Jett, Elvis Costello, AC/DC, David Johansen, Jon Spencer, the Police, Sea Monster, Social Distortion, PJ Harvey, Offspring, Bruce Springsteen, Rancid and Television.

- Patti Smith played two sets a night, four times a week, for seven consecutive weeks before she was signed by Clive Davis to Arista Records.

- The Damned was the first UK punk band to play at CBGB.

- In 1977, CB's installed a state-of-the-art sound system which they paid off in 1994.

- Talking Heads debuted "Psycho Killer."

- Living Colour played 41 consecutive Monday nights before getting signed.

- Patti Smith was the last performer to play CBGB.

- The club was completely gutted by Hilly Kristal and he removed the stage, bar and chairs, even the toilets and urinals. Everything is in storage as we await a new location, which will incorporate the old artifacts and fixtures. Some was displayed in an exhibit at the *Rock and Roll Hall of Fame Annex* in Soho in New York City.

- Hilly Kristal, founder and owner of CBGB, died on August 28, 2007, at the age of 75.

Today the site is the location of John Varvatos clothing boutique. The store has left portions of CB's original walls complete with graffiti, posters, flyers and stickers. The awning remains eerily familiar to CB's original. Next door in the former CBGB Gallery is the Morrison Hotel Gallery, which exhibits rock n' roll photographs.

JOEY RAMONE PLACE
2nd Street @ Bowery

On November 30, 2003, at 1:00 pm, the City of New York renamed 2nd Street and Bowery *Joey Ramone Place*. It was the perfect location—just one block north of CBGB and just down the street from Arturo Vegas "Ramones loft," which he shared with Joey and Dee Dee. This is also the block where Roberta Bayley photographed the band for *Punk* magazine in a garden/playground on East 2nd Street. That picture by Roberta became the cover for the Ramones debut album.

GREAT GILDERSLEEVES
331 Bowery

This seedy former metal club was located one block north of CBGB in the Bowery. The club mostly booked metal cover bands. Their booking policy loosened in February of 1983, as punk band Minor Threat played here. Diversity followed, with bands like Black Flag/Henry Rollins, Norman Nardini and the Tigers, and Sam and Dave packing the sweaty confines. Great Gildersleeves is also the place where the "secret" club gig by PIL took place. The place held about 500 people and was known for its great sightlines.

ANDERSON THEATER
66 2nd Avenue

This was a former Yiddish and Vaudeville theater that had a capacity of 1,734

people. On December 27, 1977, it became CBGB's Second Avenue Theater. Performing that night were the Talking Heads, the Shirts and Tuff Darts. On December 28, 1977, the Dictators and the Dead Boys played. On November 23, 1970, the Grateful Dead played a Hells Angels benefit here. It was billed as *Hells Angels Awakening For the Living*. On February 17, 1968, Janis Joplin and Big Brother, the Holding Company enjoyed their New York City debut here. Also performing at the Anderson were B.B. King, the Yardbirds, Moby Grape and Patti Smith.

JACKSON POLLOCK
Apartment, 46 East 8th Street

Born Paul Jackson Pollock on January 28, 1912, in Cody, Wyoming, this painter became a very influential force in the abstract expressionist movement. He moved into this apartment in 1931 with his brothers Charles and Sande, and resided here again from 1943–1945 with his artist wife Lee Krasner. Lee Krasner's first painting studio was nearby at 51 East 9th Street.

They moved to their small homestead, the Springs, on Long Island in November of 1945. The Springs location is now the *Pollock-Krasner House and Study Center*. Jackson Pollock died in a car accident not far from the Springs on August 11, 1956. Also in the car were Edith Metzger, who also died, and Pollock's girlfriend Ruth Kligman, who survived.

ARTURO VEGA/RAMONES
"Rock n' Roll High School"
Loft, 6 East 2nd Street

Arturo Vega began working for the Ramones in 1974, acting as their creative and lighting director. He also created the band's "American Eagle" logo.

Jean-Michel Basquiat art studio, 2008

Arturo's loft became the official Ramones headquarters, often doubling as a place to hold interviews or do photo shoots. Joey and Dee Dee moved into the loft in 1975. Joey Ramone lived here when he wrote "Rock n' Roll High School" and "I Want You Around." The movie *Rock n' Roll High School* was produced by Roger Corman and was released on August 24, 1979. The soundtrack also included songs by Chuck Berry, "School Days," Alice Cooper, "School's Out" and Devo, "Come Back Jonee."

PALLADIUM
140 East 14th Street

Originally called the Academy of Music, this is where The Band recorded their *Rock of Ages* album on New Year's Eve, 1972. It later became the Palladium, and it was here that the Clash album *London Calling* was photographed. The Rolling Stones played here in 1978 as part of a radio promotion by WNEW-FM. Iron Maiden also performed for a radio broadcast here in 1982. Plenty of great shows took place here, including those by the Ramones, Frank Zappa, the Jam, UFO and many others. It was said the Beastie Boys wrote "Fight For Your Right" at this club one night. Capacity for a club show was a few thousand. It became a popular dance club in the '80s. New York University bought the building in 2001, and it remains a part of the NYU campus.

JEAN-MICHEL BASQUIAT
Apartment/Studio
57 Great Jones Street

Andy Warhol once owned this two-story carriage house located off the Bowery. In the fall of 1983, artist Jean-Michel Basquiat moved into the property at a rent of $4,000 a month. He was often late with his payments because of his drug habit and his extravagance. Jean-Michel Basquiat died of a drug overdose at 57 Great Jones Street on August 12, 1988 at the age of 27. At the time of his death, Christie's Auction House in New York City claims Basquiat left behind 917 drawings, 25 sketchbooks, 85 prints and 171 paintings. Basquiat is buried in Green-Wood Cemetery in Brooklyn, New York.

ROBERT MAPPLETHORPE
Apartment/Studio, 24 Bond Street

American photographer Robert Mapplethorpe resided here for most of the '80s. Best known for his black and white

Iggy Pop at Tower Records in the East Village

archive. Ginsberg passed away on April 5, 1997, at the age of 70, just a few months after this purchase. The cause of death was a heart attack due to severe liver disease.

LONE STAR CAFE
61 5th Avenue @ East 13th Street

This is the original location of this country/rock bar, which opened in 1977. It certainly was a piece of Texas right in Manhattan. As you approached the club you would notice perched atop the roof a 41-foot, 3,000-pound green iguana! Levon Helm of The Band played here in 1988 and was joined on stage by Bob Dylan. James Brown and Jerry Lee Lewis also played here and Keith Richards joined ex-Rolling Stone Mick Taylor on stage one night. The club closed in 1989 and relocated Uptown under the name Lone Star Roadhouse.

portraits and male nudes, he sparked national attention with his Portfolio X series. It was explicit in nature and contained a self-portrait of a bullwhip in his anus. Mapplethorpe also did the cover shot of Patti Smith's *Horses* album. He died on March 9, 1989, at the age of 42 due to complications from the AIDS virus.

ALLEN GINSBERG
Apartment, 408 East 10th Street

Allen Ginsberg was born in New Jersey on June 3, 1926. While attending Columbia University in Manhattan, Ginsberg met many people who went on to influence the Beat Generation, including Jack Kerouac, Neal Cassady and William Burroughs. This was one of Ginsberg's many East Village apartments. He lived here for 10 years from 1965–1975.

ALLEN GINSBERG
Apartment, 170 East 2nd Street

Ginsberg lived here from 1958–1961, while editing *Naked Lunch* and planning the psychedelic revolution with Timothy Leary.

ALLEN GINSBERG
Death Site
404 East 14th Street

In 1996, Allen Ginsberg bought a loft in this six-story tenement building with the money he received from Stanford University, due to the sale of his huge

YIPPIE CENTER AND MUSEUM
9 Bleecker Street

The counterculture/anti-war group "Yippies" (Youth International Party) had their office here on Bleecker Street after moving from Union Square in 1973. Recently the location was turned into a Yippie Museum and a center to fight the transmission of AIDS. Abbie Hoffman and Jerry Rubin created the Yippie Party in 1966. The museum continues to preserve the history of the Yippies.

TENTH STREET COFFEE HOUSE
78 East 10th Street

During the '50s, East 10th Street was the center of the Lower East Side art scene. Mickey Ruskin owned this coffee shop. Mickey later opened the legendary Max's Kansas City on Park Avenue South.

PEACE EYE BOOKSTORE
383 East 10th Street

Ed Sanders, a poet, activist and member of the New York band the Fugs, opened this store in 1964 in an old kosher butcher shop. It was a very hip store for the time and represented the belief that anything could be sold as "literary curiosities." Some of the items sold included Allen Ginsberg's cold-cream jars and a framed collection of pubic hair from poets. This store became the center of activity for musicians, activists and poets. Police raided the store in January of 1966 and cited Sanders with possession of lewd and obscene literature. The ACLU defended him, and he won the case, but nothing that the police confiscated was returned, and that loss proved too much to continue with the business.

RICHARD HELL/ALLEN GINSBERG
Apartment, 437 East 12th Street

Richard Hell of Television, the Heartbreakers, the Voidoids and author of the punk anthem "Blank Generation" lived in this building for over 30 years. Allen Ginsberg also lived in this building on the fifth floor for nearly 20 years from 1975–1996, until he bought his loft on 14th Street.

ROB ZOMBIE
Apartment
263 East 10th Street

A former production assistant on *Pee Wee's Playhouse* in the late '80s and student of New York's Parsons School of Design, Rob Zombie (born Robert Cummings Jr.) found greater success fronting the band White Zombie. He later enjoyed a solo career as a psychobilly horror rocker, film director and author.

NEW PILGRIM THEATER
240 East 3rd Street

The *Music for Millions Festival* took place here on September 18, 1981, and featured Sonic Youth, Y Pants and the Misguided.

51X
51 2nd Avenue

Graffiti art began as an underground movement many years ago, but the form that we are most familiar with was created in the late '60s in New York City. 51X was an art gallery in the East Village that really popularized graffiti art during the '80s in New York. Pop artist Keith Haring, and grafitti artist Jean-Michel Basquiat displayed artwork here.

Iggy, Ice-T and me in 2003

47

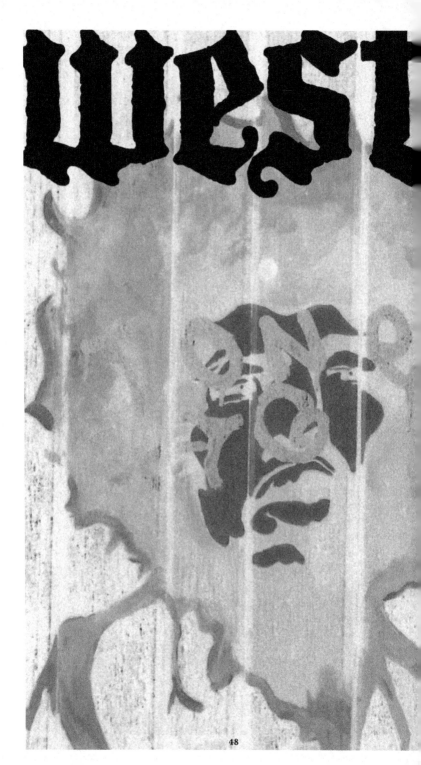

village

Greenwich Village. Just the name invokes thoughts of Bohemia, creativity, coffee houses and rebellion. Once a haven of starving artists, Beat writers, poets and musicians, today it is home to some of the trendiest restaurants, bars and expensive housing in the city. Once a marshland, the neighborhood officially became a village in 1712. Greenwich Village, often just called the West Village, was the focus of the Beat Generation of the '50s. Jack Kerouac, Allen Ginsberg, William Burroughs and Dylan Thomas considered Greenwich Village a central location in their writings. It became home of the folk generation of the '60s, as Bob Dylan emerged from the area's clubs and coffee houses. Over the last two decades many of the starving artists and musicians have moved from the West Village, as the high cost of living has driven them to other boroughs, however the West Village is now home to some of the most well-known movie stars, restaurants, galleries and venues in the world.

The arch at Washington Square Park

The legendary Bottom Line, 2003

WASHINGTON SQUARE PARK
Waverly Place @ 5th Avenue

Before it became Washington Square Park, this piece of land was known as Washington Military Parade Grounds. In the 1700s, this was nothing more than marshland surrounding the Minetta Brook. When New York City was still vastly underdeveloped, this was used as a burial ground for slaves and yellow-fever victims. The remains of more than 20,000 people are resting under the park. Nearly 10 acres in size, it wasn't known as Washington Square Park until the 1850s. The arch is widely recognized as the entrance to the West Village and was originally built about one block north of where it stands now. The

Washington Square Hotel, 2008

claim was the arch was built for the rich who lived north of the park, not for the immigrants to the south. The cost was just under $3,000. Today Washington Square Park is a gathering spot for NYU students, sunbathers, chess players, street performers and musicians.

There was a time in 1961 when the mayor of NYC, Robert Wagner, imposed a curfew on those "noisy folk musicians" who were playing in the park. When things like this happen in New York, usually there is negative feedback—so needless to say a minor riot occurred, and about a dozen people were arrested. Future mayor Ed Koch, a lawyer at the time, was chosen to represent the folk singers and appeal the curfew. He won. In the '60s, Bob Dylan and other folk musicians gathered here in the park on Sunday afternoons for their traditional "hoots," which were a bunch of folk

musicians gathering to play their music. Also, on April 18, 1993, David Lee Roth approached an undercover police officer in the park and tried to purchase $10.00 worth of weed. Roth was arrested for what he called "$10.00 worth of Jamaican bunk, maan."

WASHINGTON SQUARE HOTEL
163 Waverly Place

The 160-room Washington Square Hotel is one of the few family-owned hotels in New York City. It was previously called the Earle Hotel, and it was basically a flophouse for starving artists. When Bob Dylan first moved to New York City, he was a resident of the hotel, staying in room 305. Ramblin' Jack Elliot was a resident in room 312. Bo Diddley had also been a frequent guest of the Washington Square Hotel. Today the hotel is one of New York's finest, evoking the charm of Paris in the '30s.

BOTTOM LINE
15 West 4th Street

The Bottom Line was a West Village landmark for over 25 years. It was opened in February 1974 by partners Stanley Sandowsky and Allen Pepper. They gutted the old Red Garter Theater, which was on this site. According to Stanley and Allen, they turned the shell into a "theater inside a nightclub."

The Bottom Line always featured two sets nightly at 7:30 and 10:00 pm. Patti Smith and Elvin Bishop were the only two performers to add a third show due to high ticket demand. Those shows began at 2:00 am. The Bottom Line operated as a cash-only business. No credit cards were accepted, which made it difficult if you were entertaining a table of record-industry people. Many times while entertaining, I would leave the club and hit an ATM so that the party could continue. Walking around the West Village looking for an ATM sucked.

The Bottom Line capacity was nearly 400 people, and when it first opened it was referred to as "the Mini-Fillmore." They installed a state-of-the-art sound system complete with eight JBL speakers over the stage costing roughly $40,000. La Belle rocked the pre-opening party, but the official opening night was February 12, 1974, with Dr. John headlining. Stevie Wonder and Johnny Winter joined Dr. John on stage for an incredible jam session. In the crowd that night were Mick Jagger, Carly Simon, Charles Mingus and Don Kirshner.

On April 21, 1974, the New York Dolls played the club for the first time. They proceeded to completely trash their dressing room, resulting in the owners banning the Dolls forever. Years later David Johansen became a regular fixture at the club with his many rock personalities, like Buster Poindexter, and his blues band the Harry Smiths. Ex-New York Doll, Sylvain Sylvain played the club with his band in June of 1991. Bob Marley jammed with Taj Mahal at the Bottom Line on October 7, 1974. On June 30, 1975, legendary blues great Muddy Waters was headlining when Bob Dylan joined him onstage.

On August 13, 1975, Bruce Springsteen began a five-night run at the Bottom Line, debuting material from Born to Run. The first night was broadcast on WNEW radio. It was electrifying, and most people agree that a legend was born during those five nights. Bottom Line co-owner Stanley Sandowsky was quoted by the New York Daily News in 1984 as saying, "months after Bruce played here there was still a spirit in the place."

Other performers who have played the Bottom Line include Bo Diddley, Ronnie Spector, Warren Zevon, Television, Cheap Trick, Lou Reed, the Cars, Santana, Devo, the Dictators, Elvis Costello, the Police, Billy Joel, Donovan and, on May 10 and 11, 1976, the Ramones. The Bottom Line closed in 2003 when its landlord, New York University, demanded the owners cover their back rent. When they failed to repay the due rent, the university closed the club. It is now part of the NYU campus.

BITTER END
147 Bleecker Street

The Bitter End was opened in 1961 by former painter, designer and booking agent Paul Colby. It's one of the longest continuously operated music venues in

Bitter End, 2007

the United States. So many great bands and artists have played here, including Les Paul; Jackson Browne; Billy Joel; Dr. John; Little Feat; Neil Young; Stevie Wonder; Billy Preston; Peter, Paul and Mary, Van Morrison; David Crosby; Bo Diddley; Sam and Dave; Cass Elliot of the Mamas and the Papas and many more. Even comedians like Woody Allen and Bill Cosby have performed here. In the summer of 1975, Bob Dylan played the Bitter End with Patti Smith, Bobby Neuwirth and Ramblin' Jack Elliot before hitting the road for his infamous *Rolling Thunder Revue* tour.

The Bitter End is also where many artists have recorded live albums, such as Arlo Guthrie, Pete Seeger, The Isley Brothers and Curtis Mayfield. The original location of the Bitter End was at 31 Bleecker Street.

BLEECKER BOB'S/NITE OWL
118 West 3rd Street

Bleecker Bob's is one of the oldest record shops in New York City, and it certainly has that old-school feel with its uneven hardwood floors and hand-made CD/LP dividers. While the prices vary from reasonable to steep, Bleecker Bob's is a good place to find those out-of-print or rare albums. This location was the former home of the '60s rock club the Nite Owl, where John Sebastian and the Lovin' Spoonful and the Mamas and the Papas performed. Opened in 1967 by Bob Plotnik, the original location was on Bleecker Street.

CAFE BIZARRE
106 West 3rd Street

Cafe Bizarre was old bohemia in the '60s, a club with fishnet on the walls, sawdust on the floor, espresso and coffee for the customers and drinks made of ice cream and coconut fizz. In mid-December of 1965, the Velvet Underground played their first regular gig here. They performed two sets per night for a total of $5.00. They didn't mind because they felt they had a chance to really work on their songs in a live setting. The club was very loud partly because it was long and narrow and the stage was level with the floor. At one show, the Velvet Underground played so loud that a patron told the band "if they played that

Front door at Electric Lady Studios, 2008

song again that loud he'd beat the shit of them." The Velvet Underground not only played the song again, they played it twice as loud. You must love their style and attitude!

It was here that Andy Warhol first heard and fell in love with the Velvet Underground. Paul Morrissey suggested to John Cale that Andy should be their manager for a number of reasons. One being that Warhol was setting up this multimedia-type event at the Dom on St. Marks Place in a few months, and it would be a great scene for the Velvet Underground to be a part of. When Warhol mentioned that he never managed a rock band before, they said, that's cool, because if you're our manager our fans will then believe what we do on stage is art. So they set up a company called Warvel (WARhol/VELvet) and all money earned was directed to the company. A 25% cut was deducted for the company, and the Velvet Underground received the rest. Warvel then became responsible for setting up gigs, buying musical gear, paying the rent, etc. It

worked out well because Andy found a band that would attract a very different crowd that dressed as dark as the Velvet Underground's music and attitude. Warhol later went on to design the banana cover and produce the Velvet Underground's debut. That album is one of the most influential rock records of all time.

CAFE AU GO GO
152 Bleecker Street

Praised for its fine acoustics and intimacy (capacity 210), the Cafe Au Go Go played a very important role in the New York City rock and folk movement. Bruce Springsteen's high school band the Castilles played here in 1966. Cream with Eric Clapton played a gig here in 1967. The Grateful Dead played here 13 times over two years, the first time on June 1, 1967 and the last time on October 1, 1969. John Lee Hooker released a live album from his 1966 perfornance here called *Live at Cafe Au Go Go*. It featured Muddy Waters and his band backing John Lee. Many consider it to be one of the greatest live blues recordings ever. Other musicians who have played here include Bob Dylan, Joni Mitchell, Chuck Berry and Richie Havens.

BUDDY HOLLY/BREVOORT HOTEL
11–15 5th Avenue @ 9th Street

The Brevoort Hotel, built in 1854, was the very first hotel to be built on 5th Avenue. The hotel was converted to apartments in 1946 and demolished in 1953, only to be rebuilt and named Brevoort Apartments. Buddy Holly lived here for a short time from 1958–1959. It was here that Buddy Holly recorded his infamous *Apartment Tapes*, with just his voice, a guitar and an Ampex tape recorder. The songs on that tape were "Smokey Joe's Cafe," "What to Do," "Crying, Waiting, Hoping," "That's What They Say," "Learning the Game" and "Peggy Sue Got Married."

NINTH CIRCLE
139 West 10th Street

Mickey Ruskin opened the Ninth Circle in 1962, and quickly the local artists were patronizing it. Prior to the Ninth Circle, Mickey owned two other coffee shops, the 10th Street Coffee House and Les Deux Megots on East 7th Street. In 1965, Mickey opened Max's Kansas City on Park Avenue South.

ELECTRIC LADY STUDIOS
52 West 8th Street

The famed Electric Lady Studios is a four-story brownstone that was a very big dance venue in the '40s called the Village Barn where guests would dance to hillbilly songs beneath funky chandeliers made out of milk pails. Employees wearing red-checkered shirts would serve the refreshments. It later became known as the Generation Club, and in the '60s. Sly and the Family Stone played their first gig here. In 1968, Jimi Hendrix was in the market to buy some New York City real estate, and he was

Caffe Reggio the home of the "Original Cappuccino"

looking at owning his own nightclub. He was very interested in the Generation Club and decided to pay the asking price of $50,000, however, we all know about Jimi's long hours in the studio by evidence of the many recordings that surfaced after his death. Hendrix loved to jam and would routinely rent blocks of recording time in studios solely for that purpose. Around the time of his real estate shopping, it was pointed out to Hendrix that he was spending upwards of $300,000 a year on studio time. Jimi then decided that rather than rent studio space he would build his own studio.

During the early months of 1970, construction began on studios A and B. The other floors were used as office space, and Hendrix had a part-time apartment on the third floor. Hendrix invested nearly $1 million in the studio. He designed the ground floor in the shape of a guitar. He soundproofed the entire studio because of the constant rumblings of a nearby subway line. He made sure it was completely waterproof because of the flood-prone Minetta Stream, which still flows underneath. Electric Lady Studios took about seven months to complete, and when it opened on August 27, 1970, Hendrix was the first artist to own and operate his own recording studio.

The original façade of the studio was very cool; it had a distinctive curved brick entrance which was demolished in 1997 as the new landlord opted for a more modern-looking front. The New York Landmark Society unsuccessfully tried to stop the renovation.

The building just happened to be up for landmark status in the year 2000, only three years after it was demolished.

The number of musicians that have recorded here are endless, but some of them include AC/DC, the Rolling Stones, Led Zeppelin, Van Halen, Aerosmith, B.B. King, Chuck Berry, Elvis Costello, the Clash, John Lennon and the White Stripes.

Sadly, Jimi Hendrix passed away in London on September 18, 1970, just a few weeks after the studio opened. Jimi's family brought his body back to Seattle, Washington, and buried him in Greenwood Memorial Park.

JIMI HENDRIX
Apartment, 55 West 8th Street

Jimi had plenty of apartments to crash in during his time in New York City. This apartment was right across the street from Electric Lady Studios, so he found it to be very convenient.

KIM'S MUSIC AND VIDEO UNDERGROUND
144 Bleecker Street

Kim's Underground sells CDs, books, posters and plenty of independent, foreign and cult movie DVDs, all categorized by director, genre or country. In

Entrance to Bob Dylan's West 4th Street apartment

The original Fat Black Pussycat

the movie *Desperately Seeking Susan*, Madonna's movie boyfriend played by (Aidan Quinn) held down a job at this location. The store has since been closed.

CAFFE REGGIO
119 McDougal Street

Caffe Reggio opened in 1927 and serves espresso from a one-of-a-kind chrome and bronze machine that was built in 1902. Plenty of musicians from next door at Cafe Wha? would stop by to sip a coffee, including Bob Dylan, Jimi Hendrix and Bruce Springsteen. Movies that had parts filmed here include *The Godfather 2*, *Serpico* and *Shaft*. And before he was elected President of the United States, John F. Kennedy gave a speech in front of Caffe Reggio. Why not stop by and get yourself a Double Espresso Romano with Amaretto?

THE LOVIN' SPOONFUL/ALBERT HOTEL
University Place @ 10th Street

The Lovin' Spoonful first started performing in Greenwich Village in 1965, one year after John Sebastian saw the Beatles perform on *The Ed Sullivan Show*. Sebastian was born in Greenwich Village on March 17, 1944. In 1964, the band resided at the Albert Hotel. They would frequently jam in the basement of the hotel getting ready for their Greenwich Village club gigs, probably at the Nite Owl Cafe. In 1965, the band was signed to the Kama Sutra label. Their debut contained such hits as "Do You Believe in Magic" and "Did You Ever Have to Make up Your Mind."

THE COMMONS/FAT BLACK PUSSYCAT
McDougal Street and Minetta Lane

Originally, the Fat Black Pussycat was called the Commons. On an April afternoon in 1962, Bob Dylan sat in the Fat Black Pussycat drinking coffee playing his acoustic guitar and started to write. A few hours later he had finished writing "Blowin' in the Wind." Afterwards Bob headed to Gerde's Folk City and played the song for that evening's performer, Gil Turner, who performed it live.

ROLLING STONES
Flatbed Truck Concert
12th Street @ 5th Avenue

On May 1, 1975, the Rolling Stones staged one of the greatest promotional events in the history of rock n' roll. At noon, radio stations all over the United States announced that tickets for the

Rolling Stones' *Tour of the Americas* were going on sale immediately. The Stones were to hold a press conference that afternoon at Feathers Restaurant on 9th Street and 5th Avenue in the West Village, however, at 12:30 pm, the Rolling Stones instead announced their 1975 tour while rolling down 5th Avenue on a flatbed truck, playing "Brown Sugar" and throwing handbills to the crowd. The

press was shocked, and they ran onto the street shouting at the band, "You promised us an interview," to which the Stones replied, "Fuck you." Even though it lasted only 10 minutes, I was an event that will be hard to duplicate. It was reported that 1.5 million tickets were purchased within 48 hours in the U.S. alone. It also happened to be Ronnie Wood's first outing with the Stones.

GERDE'S FOLK CITY
11 West 4th Street @ Mercer Street

This was the original location of Gerde's Folk City. In the early '60s just about every folk artist played here. Bob Dylan played his first professional gig here on April 11, 1961, opening for John Lee Hooker. In September of the same year, Robert Shelton of *The New York Times* reviewed Dylan's September 26th performance. That review created Dylan's reputation. Replacing the original building and address is a somewhat unattractive large building housing the Hebrew Union College.

Cafe Wha?, 2008

FAT BLACK PUSSYCAT/GERDE'S FOLK CITY
130 West 3rd Street

Gerdes moved their operation here in the late '60s which was formerly the Kettle of Fish and recently once again renamed the Fat Black Pussycat. The back room documents its history, dating back to the 50s, with paintings and pictures.

BOB DYLAN
Apartment, 94 McDougal Street

After living in Woodstock, New York during the late '60s, Bob Dylan returned to the city and moved into this beautiful townhouse in 1970. Dylan lived here for a few years, but, like any celebrity living in the public eye in the heart of the West Village, he experienced problems—like people rummaging through his garbage cans. One guy in particular, AJ Weberman, made Dylan's life miserable, as he would constantly collect Dylan's trash. This situation came to a boiling point after Dylan kicked Weberman's ass on the street outside the townhouse. Dylan packed it up shortly after that, and in 1973 moved his family to Malibu, California.

GASLIGHT CAFE/KETTLE OF FISH/ SCRAP BAR
114 McDougal Street

The Gaslight Cafe opened in 1958 in the basement of this building. It was often referred to as a "basket house" because the customers passed around a basket to collect money to pay the performers. The original site of the Kettle of Fish on the second floor of this building. Bob Dylan's "Masters of War" premiered at the Gaslight Cafe. Jimi Hendrix and Eric Clapton jammed here together in 1967. In 1972, Bruce Springsteen "auditioned" for Columbia Records at the Gaslight Cafe.

Bob Dylan's McDougal Street apartment

The Kettle of Fish was one of many bar/ folk hangouts for musicians in the '60s. It's gone through many changes since those days.

In the '80s, the Scrap Bar took over the former Gaslight Cafe location in the basement. It was a great rock n' roll bar and a frequent hangout for metalheads. It was a favorite party spot for Guns N' Roses and many female porn stars.

BOB DYLAN
First Apartment, 161 West 4th Street

When Bob Dylan first moved to New York City in 1961, he moved into this apartment building on West 4th Street. After recording his debut album, *Bob Dylan*, and his then girlfriend Suze Rotolo moved in. The apartment was a one-bedroom railroad flat, which he rented for $80.00 a month. Below his apartment was Bruno's Spaghetti House.

BAGEL RESTAURANT
170 West 4th Street

After playing in the West Village clubs all night, Dylan would head back to his apartment on West 4th Street. But when morning came, Dylan would usually head to the Bagel Restaurant for some breakfast or lunch. Today it's a Spanish restaurant called "Las Ramblas."

THE FREEWHEELIN' BOB DYLAN
ALBUM COVER
Jones Street between
Bleecker Street and West 4th Street

On May 27, 1963, Columbia Records released The Freewheelin' Bob Dylan. For the cover of the album, Bob Dylan and Suze Rotolo were photographed walking together on Jones Street towards Bleecker Street. The album contained such classic hits as "Blowin' in the Wind," "Masters of War" and "Don't Think Twice, It's Alright."

CEDAR TAVERN
82 University Place
Original @ 24 University Place

The Cedar Tavern was a legendary West Village bar that was a one-time hangout for Jackson Pollock, Jack Kerouac and Allen Ginsberg. The original location of the Cedar was at 24 University Place. Bob Dylan, Bobby Neuwrith and D.A. Pennebaker met here to discuss the proposed filming of the Don't Look Back movie.

John and Yoko's pre-Dakota apartment

CAFE WHA?
115 McDougal Street

At one time during the early '60s, Cafe Wha?, much like the Commons/Fat Black Pussy Cat, was described as a "seedy basket house" where artists would play for tips collected from passing a bucket through the crowd.

On January 24, 1961, Bob Dylan arrived in New York City and was not only greeted by very cold weather but also by Cafe Wha? owner Manny Roth. Yes, Manny is David Lee Roth's uncle. Manny let Dylan play a few Woody Guthrie songs during the club's nightly "Hootenanny." After Dylan was done he was overheard saying that the crowd "flipped over me, man," and he asked Roth if he could get some cash. Roth ended up giving Dylan $1.50. Bob Dylan would later write a song about that night and the bitterly cold New York winter called "Talkin' New York."

On July 5, 1966, Chas Chandler, the bass player for the Animals, went to Cafe Wha? to check out Jimi Hendrix and the Blue Flames. He was tipped off on the gig from model girlfriend to the stars, Linda Keith, who was Jimi's foxy lady at the time. The first song Hendrix played that night was "Hey Joe." Chandler was completely blown away by Jimi's style and guitar playing and persuaded Hendrix to go to London where he proceeded to become a star.

Bruce Springsteen was also a regular customer during the '60s folk nights and it's said this is where he met Little Steven Van Zandt. Many famous people frequented Cafe Wha? and some even worked here. Mary Travers of Peter, Paul and Mary was a waitress here before joining the group. And Tiny Tim hung

Kenny's Castaways on Bleecker Street, 2008

out with a young Bob Dylan, playing for basket collections.

FRANK ZAPPA
Apartment, 180 Thompson Street

Frank Zappa lived here during 1967–1968. During his stay on Thompson Street, Zappa wrote some great albums, including *Lumpy Gravy, We're Only In It for the Money, Uncle Meat*, and his '50s tribute, *Ruben and the Jets*.

KENNY'S CASTAWAYS
157 Bleecker Street

Kenny's Castaways was founded by Patrick Kenny in 1967 and quickly became the place to play, along with Max's. The original location was on the Upper East Side at 211 East 84th Street. Kenny's certainly hosted a lot of great moments, like when Bruce Springsteen debuted the E Street Band for one week in 1973. The New York Dolls played at the Uptown location, and rock photographer Bob Gruen shot some film of the Dolls at Kenny's, which later turned up on the DVD *All Dolled Up*.

After a rent dispute Uptown, Patrick moved his venue to Greenwich Village. The Smithereens were the house band in 1980, and Phish played their first New York City show here in 1988. Other performers that played here include Aerosmith, Deborah Harry and Patti Smith.

In the late 1800s, this was the site of a bar called the Slide, with the only light being that from gas-lit lamps. The city's newspaper, *The New York Herald*, was unable to find words to describe the orgies taking place here with men dressed as women, but they were quoted as saying the "scene was beyond description." The police closed the Slide in 1892. Kenny's Castaways however has been going strong for over 40 years.

GARRICK THEATER
152 Bleecker Street

Andy Warhol debuted *Blue Movie* here in 1969—a movie billed as a "film about the Vietnam War and what we can do about it." The first 35 minutes featured a couple engaged in foreplay while say-

Sid Vicious death site

ing nothing about the war. But perhaps that was the point: to make love not war. Other Andy Warhol/Paul Morrissey related films were also screened here including *Flesh* and *Bike Boy*.

SULLIVAN HALL/LION'S DEN
214 Sullivan Street

The Lion's Den opened in 1990 and has a capacity of about 400 people. They have a very good sound system, and over the years Ben Folds, New Found Glory and Dashboard Confessional have used it. The name was recently changed to Sullivan Hall.

TERRA BLUES
149 Bleecker Street

Terra Blues opened in 1990 and is one of the few blues clubs in New York City. Most acoustic sets begin about 7:00 pm, and then the bands plug in around 10:00 pm. Years ago it was a very popular drag bar called the Crazy Horse Cafe. On the street level during the '80s was a tribute-band bar called the Rock n' Roll Cafe.

BACK FENCE
155 Bleecker Street

Established in 1945, this club features many genres of music. Every Sunday afternoon they host an open mic poetry reading.

SAN REMO
93 McDougal Street @ Bleecker Street

Opened in 1923, this place was often considered a literary bar in the '50s and '60s. It became a popular spot for the Beats and Andy Warhol's Factory crowd. The San Remo was referred to in Jack Kerouac's *The Subterraneans* and was a hangout for the original Beat poets, William Burroughs, Allen Ginsberg, Jack Kerouac and Gregory Corso. Jackson Pollock and Tennessee Williams were also regulars.

IZZY YOUNG
Folklore Center
110 McDougal Street

Founded in 1957 by Izzy Young, the Folklore Center was a haunt for many folk musicians in New York City. It was a great store where people could find books, magazines and music relating to the folk scene. Bob Dylan spent many days here writing and playing his guitar in the back room.

VILLAGE GATE/CHIP MONCK
Apartment,160 Bleecker Street @ Thompson Street

Art D'Lugoff opened the Village Gate in the late '50s as a jazz club. So many great musicians have played here, including John Coltrane, Duke Ellington and Dizzy Gillespie. In 1961, Nina Simone recorded a live album here called *At the Village Gate*. Aretha Franklin made her New York City debut at this club. Also Chip Monck (born Edward Herbert Beresford Monck), the lightng and stage manager of the *Woodstock Festival* in 1969, had a basement apartment in this building in the early '60s. It was in that apartment that Bob Dylan wrote "A Hard Rain's Gonna Fall" in September of 1962.

Original site of the Lone Star Cafe as it looked in 2008

LOU REED
Apartment, 55 Christopher Street

Lou Reed has lived in many apartments in New York City, but he resided here at the time the album *Rock n Roll Animal* was recorded. The album was recorded on December 21, 1973, at New York's Academy of Music.

SID VICIOUS
Death Site, 63 Bank Street

Sid Vicious was released from jail on February 1, 1979, after posting bond on charges that he killed girlfriend Nancy Spungen at the Hotel Chelsea. After release, he was thrown a party by a former girlfriend at this Bank Street apartment. Sid shot heroin for most of the party and passed out, never to awake

again. Sid was cremated and his ashes were sprinkled over Nancy's grave in Philadelphia, Pennsylvania.

JOHN LENNON/YOKO ONO
Apartment, 105 Bank Street

Growing tired of staying at the St. Regis Hotel in Manhattan, John Lennon and Yoko Ono moved into this West Village apartment previously owned and occupied by Lovin' Spoonful drummer Joe Butler. It was here at this apartment that John and Yoko wrote songs for the album *Sometime in New York City*. John and Yoko resided here for about two years before heading Uptown and moving into the Dakota.

The Freewheelin' Bob Dylan album cover site

Le Figaro Cafe, a favorite Beat hangout

GRACE JONES
Apartment, 166 Bank Street

Born Grace Mendoza, this actress, musician and model that we know as Grace Jones lived in this apartment building while she resided in New York City. Although she was a superb vocalist and earned a Grammy nomination for the video "One Man Show," Grace became better known for her looks and image than her music.

ROLLING STONES
"Dance Part 1"
from *Emotional Rescue*
West 8th Street @ 6th Avenue

The intro of "Dance Part 1" on *Emotional Rescue* has Mick Jagger asking, "What am I doing standing here on the corner of West 8th Street and 6th Avenue?" Perhaps he was getting Keith a Gray's Papaya hot dog!

JIMI HENDRIX
West Village Crash Pad
31 Bedford Street

Jimi Hendrix loved both the East and West Villages, but he used to crash here quite a bit in the late '60s. Hendrix referred to it as his "little hideaway," because of its hard-to-find location.

LE FIGARO CAFE
186 Bleecker Street

Le Figaro Cafe was a major West Village hangout for many Beats poets in the '50s. In the '60s it became a very important folk venue in the West Village. The site is now a Mexican restaurant. The original location opened in 1956 at 195 Bleecker Street.

WOODY GUTHRIE
Apartment, 1943
74 Charles @ Bleecker Street

Woody Guthrie was born on July 14, 1912, in Okemah, Oklahoma. He lived in many apartments in New York City, but this was the apartment where in 1943 he entertained blues great, Leadbelly. Woody's rent back in 1943 was $27.00 a month.

Woody Guthrie died of Huntington's Disease on October 3, 1967 at Creedmoor Hospital in Queens, New York. His ashes were sprinkled off the shores of Coney Island in Brooklyn. In his lifetime, Woody Guthrie wrote nearly 3,000 songs.

WOODY GUTHRIE
Apartment, 1942
148 West 14th Street

Legendary folk songwriter Woody Guthrie resided here on West 14th Street in 1942.

JIMI HENDRIX
Last New York City Apartment
59 West 12th Street

Although Jimi Hendrix died in London in September of 1971, this was his New York City apartment at the time of his death. Jimi resided in apartment 10C and was often visited by Mitch Mitchell and Billy Cox to work on new material. In addition to recording new songs for an upcoming album, Hendrix was also working on the design of Electric Lady Studios.

WHITE HORSE TAVERN
567 Hudson Street @ West 11th Street

The White Horse Tavern opened in 1880 and is probably best know as the bar where Dylan Thomas drank himself to an early death in November of 1953. The bar was a gathering spot for writers, Beat poets, artists and musicians in the '50s and '60s. The Clancy Broth-

ers often performed here in the '60s, and Bob Dylan frequently stoped by to see them play. The White Horse Tavern remains open today and is a great spot to soak up the past.

WILLIAM S. BURROUGHS
Apartment
69 Bedford Street @ Commerce Street

William Burroughs (February 5, 1914–August 2, 1997) is best known as a great novelist, painter, spoken word performer and main figure of the Beat Generation. During the five months he lived here, he was working as a private detective and tended bar. Burroughs had a second-floor furnished apartment that he lived in between 1943–1944.

WASHINGTON SQUARE ART GALLERY
100 Washington Square East

Andy Warhol began making movies in 1963. He premiered his film *Blowjob* here during March of 1964. Uncharacteristic of Warhol's later movie work, this film shot its load in 41 minutes. Warhol referred to many of his movies as experimental because, he said, "I didn't know what the fuck I was doing."

Corner of West 8th Street and 6th Avenue

Hendrix image on the door at Cafe Wha?

WETLANDS
161 Hudson Street

Wetlands was an environmental- and social-justice activist center and music club located on Hudson Street that opened in February of 1989. They fought for human, animal and earth liberation through many different avenues. Upon entering the 500-person capacity club, one of the first things you saw was a 1967 VW van. The van served as an info booth where you could get literature about environmental and social causes.

Grace Jones apartment

The bus is now in the Rock and Roll Hall of Fame and Museum in Cleveland.

While the club had a reputation as being as a "hippie haven," it actually put on some very diversified shows. In addition to the jam bands that frequently played there, they also hosted hip-hop, punk and hardcore shows. Some of the bands that have graced the stage include Rancid, Bad Brains, L7, Anti-Flag, James "Blood" Ulmer, Alex Chilton, Babes in Toyland, Bad Religion, Dave Matthews, 7 Seconds, Live, Blind Melon, Black 47 and Living Colour. Also, Pearl Jam and Sublime had their first-ever New York City shows at Wetlands. The odd placement of the stage didn't leave much room to view the band straight on; so many patrons were left hanging at the bar or watching the show from stage right. The club closed in September of 2001, but The Wetlands Activism Center remains operating. The building vas sold and converted into esidential condos.

VILLAGE VANGUARD
178 7th Avenue South

Opened in 1935 by Max Gordon, the Village Vanguard is considered one of the most influential jazz clubs in the world. It's often been called "the Carnegie Hall of Jazz"

Original Village Gate sign still adorns the building, Bleecker Street

because of its incredible acoustics. The Village Vanguard has been the site of more than 150 live albums, including those by John Coltrane and Sonny Rolins. It still holds its original capacity of 123. Miles Davis, Thelonious Monk and Charles Mingus played here numerous times, and the Village Vanguard also helped advance the career of blues great, Leadbelly.

INROADS
151 Mercer Street

Before the Arcadians changed their name to Sonic Youth in 1981, they played a gig here on January 29, 1981. Guitarist Thurston Moore came up with the name Sonic Youth, combining the names of influences Fred "Sonic" Smith of the MC5 and reggae artist Big Youth.

MOBY
Grandfather's Former Residence
33 Bleecker Street

Electronic artist Moby had a famous grandfather named Herman Melville who in 1851 wrote one of the greatest novels of all time, *Moby Dick*. Herman Melville called this his childhood home. How did you think Moby got that cool name?

Thomas was a regular at the White Horse Tavern

MCBURNEY YMCA
125 West 14th Street

This is a historic branch of the community service organization that inspired the the Village People's iconic disco hit "YMCA." The single peaked at number two on *Billboard's* Hot 100 Chart in 1978, and was from the album *Crusin'*. At one time, both Andy Warhol and Al Pacino were members of the historic McBurney YMCA. Initiation fee in 2009 was only $125.

attery park

The entire area from Houston Street to Battery Park
is made up of so many diversified and cool
neighborhoods: Soho, the Lower East Side,
Tribeca, Chinatown, Little Italy, Battery Park City
and the Financial District.
The blocks surrounding Battery Park are the center
of business and government in New York City.
It's actually the fourth-largest business district in the
United States, behind Midtown Manhattan,
Chicago's Loop and Washington D.C.
It was the third largest in the U.S. until the
September 11, 2001 terrorist attacks on the U.S.

...AND IT IS ALL FOR YOU...

Moby's place

BEASTIE BOYS/PAUL'S BOUTIQUE
99 Rivington Street

On July 25, 1989, the Beastie Boys released *Paul's Boutique*. The album contained such songs as "Shake Your Rump," "Egg Man" and "Hey Ladies." The building or business space was to be called Paul's Boutique, but as you can see by the album cover, the building was actually called Lee's Sportswear. The building eventually became an eatery called Paul's Boutique, but ceased operations in early 2007.

MOBY/TEANY
90 Rivington Street

In May of 2002, musician Moby opened a vegetarian/vegan tea-room complete with "tea-robots as mascots." The menu is plentiful with tasty treats like blueberry crumb muffins, scones, salads and sandwiches. Iced teas, hot teas, coffee and alcohol are available if you're thirsty.

ABC No Rio
56 Rivington Street

A center for arts and activism, ABC No Rio was founded in 1980. Punk band Rancid lit up the night here early in their career. The center became named ABC No Rio as a result of the previous owners, a lawyer and notary, who had a sign on the building that said "AB(ogado) C(on) NO(ta)RIO." Some lights burned out on the sign, and the lights that remained lit spelled ABC No Rio.

MERCURY LOUNGE
217 East Houston Street

This was originally a servant's quarter for the Astor family, who resided in a mansion north of Houston Street at what is now Stuyvesant Street. It later became a headstone shop. While you're getting a drink, check out the headstone on the bar's countertop. The Mercury Lounge is a premier New York rock club with a great sound system that has played host to Lou Reed, the White Stripes, Joan Jett, Bikini Kill, Luscious Jackson and Radiohead, to name a few. The room holds about 200 fans.

BOWERY BALLROOM
6 Delancey Street

In the early 1900s, this was the site of a three-story the-

Mercury Lounge, 2008

ater. This beautiful Beaux Arts building that replaced that theatre was finished just before the stock market crash of 1929. During the mid-1900s, a bunch of high-end retail stores occupied the ground floor, and much of the 1929 remnants still remain in the club. It's now the Bowery Ballroom, a fantastic room for bands to play that accommodates about 600 fans. Metallica, Coldplay, Courtney Love, the White Stripes, Dirtbombs, the Hives and Jet have all played here.

MERCER CITY ARTS CENTER
240 Mercer Street

The New York Dolls first started playing the Mercer Arts Center at the suggestion of Johnny Thunders' girlfriend Janice Cafasso. Their first gig at the Center was in June of 1972, supporting Satan and the Eternal Fire Eater and the Magic Tramps. Back in the 1800s, this was the site of the Broadway Central Hotel. The Arts Center had different rooms named after famous playwrights, such as the Mercer Bernard Shaw Arena and the Oscar Wilde Cabaret. In 1972, the Dolls had a 17-week residency in the Oscar Wilde Cabaret.

WHITE COLUMNS
325 Spring Street

This was an art gallery that held about 60–70 people at its maximum. In 1981 Thurston Moore of Sonic Youth organized a nine-day music festival here to help out underemployed experimental/noise performers that were a part of the Downtown music scene. It was billed as *The Noisefest* and ran from June 16th to June 24th. About four different acts performed each night. Those performers that were a part of the festival included Dog Eat Dog, Mofungo, Glen Branca, Chinese Puzzle and, obviously, Sonic Youth. The cost of admission for the show was $4.00.

ROBERT QUINE
Death Site, 96 Grand Street

Robert Quine, who played with Richard Hell and the Voidoids, Marianne Faithul, Brian Eno, Tom Waits and with Lou Reed on *Blue Mask*, was found dead in his fourth-floor apartment on June 5, 2004. The death was an alleged suicide and a note was found in the apartment.

VELVET UNDERGROUND
Apartment, 56 Ludlow Street

On the cusp of success in 1965, John Cale and Lou Reed shared a loft apartment at this location. The time spent here forming the Velvet Underground resulted in the bootleg *Ludlow Street Demos*. The six songs on that demo were "Venus in Furs," (15:33), "Prominent Man," (4:53), "Heroin," (13:34), "I'm Waiting for the Man," (9:50), "Wrap Your Troubles in Dreams," (15:50), and "All Tomorrow's Parties" (18:26). During those lean years, it was rumored that both John Cale and Lou Reed would eat oatmeal all day and night and donate blood to earn some cash.

PAUL SIMON/SAY ENG LOOK
Restaurant
1 East Broadway, Chinatown

Native New Yorker Paul Simon has enjoyed a long and profitable career, first with Art Garfunkel, then with a solo career. He will certainly be remembered for the hit single "Mother and Child Reunion," from his 1972 album *Paul Simon*. Paul was dining at Say Eng Look Restaurant one day, and while looking

Lou Reed and John Cale shared this apartment on Ludlow Street

at the menu Paul was inspired by a dish called "Mother and Child Reunion." It's a tasty Chinese entree, featuring chicken and eggs.

CHUNG KING HOUSE OF METAL
241 Centre Street

Located in a former Chinatown Chinese restaurant, Chung King House of Metal recording studio became aligned with some of the most influential rap recordings in history. Some of the artists that recorded here were Run DMC, LL Cool J, Public Enemy's *Fear of a Black Planet* and the Beastie Boys' *License to Ill*. As a result, Chung King became known as "The Abbey Road of Rap Music."

Bowery Ballroom, 2008

ABC No Rio, 2008

Not everyone enjoyed the studio, however. In 1989, New York City hardcore band Judge booked a three-day weekend of studio time. But they were assigned one of the least functional and desirable studios. On top of that, because of their anti-drug songs, they were given a producer who was allegedly wired on cocaine. On day two the producer never showed up, and they were given a producer who was unfamiliar with hardcore music. The album was released on vinyl and called *Chung King Can Suck It*. The credits on the album read "not produced and engineered by some cokehead loser." Today the studio is located on Varick Street in Soho.

ARLENE'S GROCERY
95 Stanton Street

Arlene's Grocery opened in 1995 and decided to keep the name of its previous tenant, a bodega. This 150-person capacity club is adjoined by a very hip and laid-back bar. It's a great room to see a band, and every Monday night they feature "Rock n' Roll Karaoke." Basically fans get on stage and sing their favorite songs in front of a great live band. Celebrities like David Bowie, Mick Jagger, Liv Tyler and others have popped by to check out some of the local bands at this Lower East Side club.

BAGGIES
71 Grand Street

This was one of the first studios in New York City that was considered ultra-professional, and they rented by the hour, pleasing many artists. Carlos Santana must have thought so, because he laid down some tracks here.

JOHNNY THUNDERS
Apartment
119 Chrystie Street, Chinatown

Born John Anthony Genzale on July 15, 1952, in Queens, Johnny Thunders and his girlfriend Janice Cafasso shared an apartment at this location above a Chinese noodle factory.

MUDD CLUB
77 White Street

The Mudd Club was a legendary '70s Downtown club opened by Steve Mass. Could a Downtown club introduce the

Arlene's Grocery, 2008

et set to a punk-rock lifestyle? The answer was yes. Punk purists would crowd this smallish club, and eager customers would line the street waiting to get in. Bands performed and DJs spun everything from garage to punk. Prior to becoming a world-famous artist, Keith Haring used to work the door at the Mudd Club.

SHIMMY DISC RECORDS
Former Office, 247 West Broadway

Often considered one of the best alternative record labels of the '90s, Shimmy Disc was the brainchild of Kramer, whose band Bongwater enjoyed success dur-

ing that time. Kramer packed up his bong and water and headed to New Jersey, where he bought himself a home.

PLATINUM ISLAND STUDIOS
676 Broadway

This is another Downtown studio where plenty of musicians recorded hit albums. Mariah Carey recorded most of her 1991 album *Emotions* here, and Michael Jackson also did some remixes of a few of his singles.

Paul's Boutique post-Beastie Boys

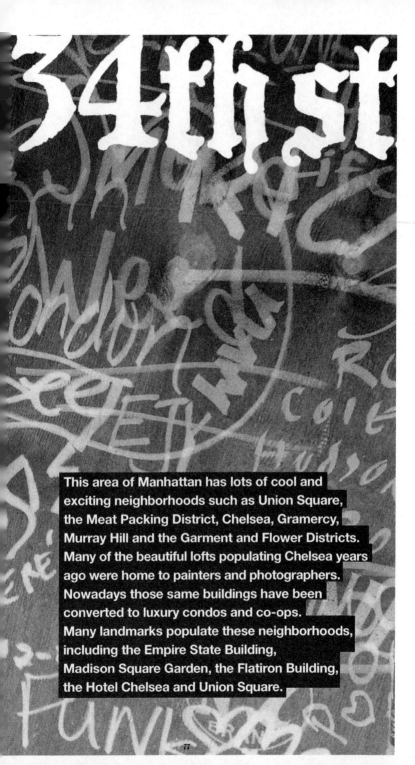

34th st

This area of Manhattan has lots of cool and exciting neighborhoods such as Union Square, the Meat Packing District, Chelsea, Gramercy, Murray Hill and the Garment and Flower Districts. Many of the beautiful lofts populating Chelsea years ago were home to painters and photographers. Nowadays those same buildings have been converted to luxury condos and co-ops.
Many landmarks populate these neighborhoods, including the Empire State Building, Madison Square Garden, the Flatiron Building, the Hotel Chelsea and Union Square.

LIVE
NUDES
LIVE
…E THEATER Co.
…O BURLESQUE CABARET
Memorial Jazz Theatre
…30 E 7th St
…IDAY 8:30
11/21
LENN…
& L…
TITS
& ASS
NIGHTLY
A SN…
B.Y.O…

Lobby of Hotel Chelsea

HOTEL CHELSEA
222 West 23rd Street

The Hotel Chelsea, or Chelsea Hotel as it's commonly referred to, was built in 1884 and was New York City's tallest building for 18 years until 1902. It served as a co-op apartment building until it went bankrupt because of rising taxes and some financial set backs. In 1905, it became a hotel.

Musicians and writers loved to stay here because of its proximity to the West Village and the Midtown publishing houses.

The list of writers that have stayed at the Chelsea reads like a who's who of literature: Arthur Miller, Allen Ginsberg, Charles Bukowski, Tennessee Williams, Gore Vidal, Jack Kerouac and Robert Hunter, among others. During the early 1900s, Mark Twain was a frequent guest of the hotel. Until his death in 1910, William Sydney Porter, better known as O. Henry, stayed here. During the '30s, Thomas Wolfe wrote *Look Homeward Angel* and *The Web and the Rock* here. On September 21, 1968, Charles R. Jackson, author of *The Lost Weekend*, committed suicide in his room. In 1953, in room 206, writer Dylan Thomas went into a coma as a result of an all-night drinking binge at the White Horse Tavern. In 1959, William Burroughs wrote *Naked Lunch* while staying at the Chelsea. Some of the many actors and directors that have stayed here include Jane Fonda, Dennis Hopper, Uma Thurman and Stanley Kubrick.

In the '60s, Andy Warhol's Factory crowd set up residence here, and it was at that time that the Chelsea began to attract more of the rock n' roll crowd. Lou Reed wrote "Walk on the Wild Side," which was about the crazy mix of Warhol characters that were staying at the hotel, such as Candy Darling and Holly Woodlawn—the girl who came from Miami, F.L.A. On August 10, 1967, the Grateful Dead played a show on the roof of the hotel. Allegedly Janis Joplin severed ties with Big Brother and the Holding Company while staying here, and during that stay she met up with Leonard Cohen and allegedly blew him

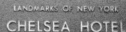

LANDMARKS OF NEW YORK

CHELSEA HOTEL

DESIGNED BY HUBERT & PIRSSON, THE CHELSEA WAS
OPENED IN 1884 AS ONE OF THE CITY'S EARLIEST
COOPERATIVE APARTMENT HOUSES. IT BECAME A
HOTEL ABOUT 1905. THE FLORID CAST IRON BALCONIES
WERE MADE BY THE FIRM OF J. B. & J. M. CORNELL.
ARTISTS AND WRITERS WHO HAVE LIVED HERE INCLUDE
ARTHUR B. DAVIES, JAMES T. FARRELL, ROBERT
FLAHERTY, O. HENRY, JOHN SLOAN, DYLAN THOMAS
AND THOMAS WOLFE.

PLAQUE ERECTED 1962 BY
THE NEW YORK COMMUNITY TRUST

A landmark plaque outside Hotel Chelsea

on an unmade bed. Grace Slick and the Jefferson Airplane wrote the song "Third Week in Chelsea" from the album *Bark* while staying here. While staying in room A17, Bob Dylan wrote the classic "Sad Eyed Lady of the Lowlands" about his wife Sara. On the 1976 album, he acknowledged it with the song "Sara."

On October 12, 1978, punk-rock's-Yoko Nancy Spungen met her maker in room 100. Allegedly Sid Vicious awoke to find her in the bathroom with a knife in her stomach. Sid was set to go to trial but overdosed on heroin and died while out on bail. Soon after that, tragic punk rockers and music fans would always request to stay in room 100. It became unbearable for the hotel staff because of the constant thefts from the room. It was years later that the hotel decided to "renovate" room 100 by knocking down the wall and joining two rooms together. So there is no more room 100 at the Chelsea. At one time, Rough Trade Records had office space in that room.

Other musicians that have stayed here include Patti Smith, Richard Hell, Tom Waits, Joni Mitchell, Jimi Hendrix and John Cale. Dee Dee Ramone was a long-time resident of the hotel, and he even wrote a novel about it called *Chelsea Horror Hotel*. Many photos from Madonna's 1992 *Sex* book were shot here. Today the Chelsea is a mixture of apartments and hotel rooms.

MOTHERS
267 West 23rd Street

This former gay bar across from the Hotel Chelsea hosted plenty of punk bands in the '70s. Peter Crowley, who

Rising Dragon Tattoos on West 23rd Street

also managed Wayne County, handled the majority of the bookings, and Mothers was often thought of as a cool alternative to playing Max's Kansas City or CBGB. Blondie and the Ramones played here in 1975. The bar also hosted Talking Heads, Wayne County, Television, the Heartbreakers, Mink De Ville and countless others. Crowley became the music director at Max's in the mid-70s, and Mothers was then bought and changed to Zepps.

RISING DRAGON TATTOOS
230 West 23rd Street

Arturo Vega was the lighting and creative director for the Ramones, and a very good abstract painter. He created the Ramones' "American Eagle" logo. Years later he had that logo tattooed on his back at Rising Dragon Tattoos in Chelsea. How ironic the shop is right next to the Hotel Chelsea, where Dee Dee Ramone lived for a number of years. Artist Darren Rosa did the tattoo on Arturo. Rising Dragon also had a second shop located at 53rd and 3rd. Hmmm, quite a coincidence.

LESTER BANGS
Apartment, 542 6th Avenue

In 1976, Lester Bangs moved to New York City to continue his work as a freelance writer. Before moving to New York City he had written over 150 reviews for *Rolling Stone* magazine between 1969 and 1973. *Rolling Stone* fired him in 1973 after a poor review of *Canned Heat*. Some of his favorite bands were the Ramones, Captain Beefheart, Roxy Music, Miles Davis, Lou Reed, Black Sabbath, Patti Smith and the New York

Dolls. It was rumored that one day during a fire in his apartment, Lester was seen running from the building clutching his PIL limited-edition box. He was also a former editor and writer for *Creem* magazine and had one album that was released on Spy Records in 1979 called *Let It Blurt Live*. On April 30, 1982, Lester Bangs was found dead in this apartment after an apparent overdose of Darvon and Valium.

ANDY WARHOL/FACTORY
2nd Location, 33 Union Square West

The second incarnation of Andy Warhol's famed Factory lasted six years, from 1968–1974. It was at this location on June 3, 1968, on the sixth floor, that Valerie Solanis shot Warhol. Warhol's crew considered Solanis a borderline stalker. She was a radical feminist writer who penned *The SCUM Manifesto*—SCUM being the acronym for Society for Cutting Up Men. Before Warhol moved to the third Factory location in 1974, he did one final painting at the Union Square Factory of his mother, who passed away in 1972.

LIMELIGHT
660 6th Avenue

Built in 1846 and originally called the Church of Holy Communion, the Limelight chain of clubs first opened in Hol-

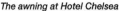
The awning at Hotel Chelsea

Madison Square Garden

lywood, Florida in the '70s. Peter Gatien opened his New York version in November 1993. It opened its doors as a disco and rock club, but during the '90s it became the place to hear industrial, techno and goth music. It was closed by the police many times in the '90s. The club reopened in 2003 under the name Avalon. I've witnessed and participated in many sins in those confessionals.

JONI MITCHELL
Apartment, 41 West 16th Street

There have been many songs written about New York City, and Joni Mitchell penned one while living in this apartment. The song is called "Chelsea Morning," and she said it was inspired by this neighborhood.

SCOTT IAN/ANTHRAX
**Father's Jewelry Company
243 West 30th Street**

Formed in 1981, New York City metal band Anthrax decided upon their name after seeing it in a biology textbook and thought it sounded evil. Before the band grew in popularity, however, founding member and guitarist Scott Ian could be found working here for his father's jewelry manufacturing company.

TRAMPS
**Original Location,
125 East 15th Street**

This was the original location of Tramps which spawned the birth of Buster Poindexter. It was a small club, and the DJs loved spinning reggae, blues and soul. The club moved to 45 West 21st Street into a space that held about 400 people. Bob Dylan played there in the late '90s as did the Ramones and Patti Smith. In 2001, it became Centro-Fly and featured guest DJs like the Chemical Brothers and Fat Boy Slim.

WILLEM de KOONING
Apartment, 156 West 22nd Street

Artist Willem de Kooning moved into this studio apartment in 1936 with then-girlfriend Juliet Browner. The apartment had no water as it was zoned for commercial use, not residential. Willem de Kooning later met Elaine Fried and they married and moved to a higher floor. The $35.00 a month rent proved to be a bit expensive for them, and they were evicted in December of 1946.

IN PAN ALLEY
8th Street between 6th Avenue and Broadway

At the beginning of the 1900s, this was the hub of music publishing in the United States. At that time, "publishing" consisted of nothing more than sheet music. The publishers would hire piano players to play the music for potential customers. The sound of the pianos all playing at once created an unusual "tinny" sound, giving the street its nickname.

MADISON SQUARE GARDEN
7th Avenue @ 33rd Street

Madison Square Garden has been called "The World's Most Famous Arena." The Garden dates back to 1879, with the first of its four eventual locations at Madison Avenue and 26th Street.

The second location of the Garden was at 23rd Street and Madison Avenue. Opening night was June 16, 1890. New York Life, the landlord of the building, decided to build its office building on the very site of the Garden, so it was to relocate again. The final event in Garden II took place in May of 1925, a boxing match between Sid Terris and Johnny Dundee.

The Garden then moved Uptown to 8th Avenue and 48th Street for its third location. With the opening of Garden III in 1925, professional hockey was introduced in New York City. In the late '50s and early '60s, 8th Avenue and Hell's Kitchen began decaying, and patrons at the Garden would rush home and forego any cocktails or dining in nearby restaurants. As a result, officials of the Garden Corporation decided to move the Garden yet again.

The new location was built on the site of the old Penn Station, which just happened to be one of most beloved buildings in all of New York. They figured that the Long Island Railroad and two different subway lines running underneath the new Garden could only benefit the patrons. Destruction of Penn Station began in 1963. As a result of the travesty of tearing down the beloved Penn Station, the Landmarks Preservation Commission was created in 1965. Now going forward, they are able to preserve historic buildings in New York.

The new Madison Square Garden officially opened on February 11, 1968. Music comprises a large part of the history of this Garden. The Rolling Stones made their first Madison Square Garden appearance on Thanksgiving Day, November 27, 1969. They played an afternoon show and a late night show. *Get Yer Ya Ya's Out* was the live album culminating from those two shows.

In January of 1969, the Doors played the Garden, and in May of that same year, Jimi Hendrix rocked the house. Janis Joplin played the Garden only once on December 19, 1969. On August 1, 1971, George Harrison invited musicians to the Garden to raise money for starving refugees. The event was billed as *The Concert for Bangladesh*, which was the first major benefit concert. Elvis played four consecutive sold-out shows in 1972. In 1974, Frank Sinatra's *Main Event* concert was broadcast live throughout the world. Also in 1974, John Lennon performed in public here for the last time, joining Elton John on stage for three songs. The Grateful Dead played the

Garden 52 times, only to be outdone by Elton John, who played the Garden for the record-breaking 53rd time on November 28, 2001. On March 25, 2007, Elton took the Garden stage for his 60th sold-out performance.

THE MUSIC BUILDING
585 8th Avenue

This was dubbed "The Music Building" because of its massive rehearsal space, 10 floors located near Manhattan's Port Authority Bus Terminal. When Generation X band-member Billy Idol first moved to New York City, it was here that he rehearsed and wrote the hit song "White Wedding." While working on her first record deal with Sire Records, Madonna frequently used the space as her crash quarters until she scored some money.

KISS
Album Cover
23rd Street @ 8th Avenue

Bob Gruen is one of rock's greate[st] photographers. In 1975, Kiss release[d] their third album *Dressed to Kill*. Bo[b] set up the album cover shot on th[e] south west corner of 23rd Street an[d] 8th Avenue.

JACK KEROUAC
On The Road
454 West 20th Street

On April 22, 1951, Jack Kerouac finishe[d] writing one of the most celebrated nov[-] els of our time called *On The Road*. In[-] spired by his drug-fueled cross-countr[y] car trips with Neal Cassidy, Keroua[c] penned *On The Road* in a mere 2[0] days in his mother's apartment on Wes[t]

Limelight as it looked in 2008

0th Street. Kerouac thus became spokesman for the Beat
Generation. To date, *On The
Road* has sold more than four
million copies.

HAMMERSTEIN BALLROOM
847 West 34th Street

What was once a Manhattan
opera house is now one of
the premier rock concert halls
in New York. It was erected in
1906, and in 1910 it became a
vaudeville hall and then a movie
theater. It also was a Freemason
Temple during the Great De-
pression. It has roughly 12,000
square feet of space and the
ceilings are 75 feet high. It holds
3,500 patrons during concerts
and has a two-tiered balcony
with seating. The orchestra pit
was removed years ago to give
the fans room to mosh. Bob
Dylan, Marilyn Manson, the
White Stripes, Audioslave and
Joey Ramone's Birthday Bash
shows have all been here.

DANCETERIA
30 West 21st Street

Danceteria had three different
locations throughout the '80s,
251 West 30th Street, 30 East
30th Street and this location off 5th
Avenue at 21st Street. This location is
probably the most famous of the three,
as the dance scene in Madonna's *Desperately Seeking Susan* was filmed
here. After moving to New York City,
Madonna worked here briefly as a coat
check girl. She handed her mix tape to
DJ Mark Kamins, and he played a few
songs for the crowd. Singer Sade also
worked at this location serving drinks to
thirsty throngs.

Max's Kansas City, 2007

JOHNNY THUNDERS
Last NYC Apartment
227 East 21st Street

This was former New York Doll and
Heartbreaker Johnny Thunders' last New
York City apartment. Thunders' pad was
directly across the street from a precinct
of the New York City Police Department. This studio walk-up apartment
was cramped with piles of cassettes, a
mattress on the floor and a wall picture
of Jesus and the Mother Mary. Thunders

died of a heroin overdose at St. Peter Guest House in New Orleans in 1991.

MAX'S KANSAS CITY
213 Park Avenue South

Max's Kansas City opened for business in December of 1965. Owner Mickey Ruskin created such a hip environment that Max's became center stage for artists, musicians and movie stars. Andy Warhol once said Max's is where Pop Art met Pop Life. Many people believe the success and amazing vibe of Max's had to do with Mickey—the diversified list of people that would show up to play and party testify to his influence. Andy Warhol, Mick Jagger, Lou Reed, Faye Dunaway, Abbie Hoffman, Salvador Dali, Truman Capote, Iggy Pop, Bebe Buell, Johnny Thunders, David Johansen, Jane Fonda, Fellini, Dennis Hopper, Robert Mapplethorpe, Allen Ginsberg, Jim Morrison and thousands of others.

Before Mickey opened Max's, he was also the owner of the Tenth Street Coffee House, the Ninth Circle on West 10th Street, Les Deux Megots on East 7th Street and the Annex in the East Village. When Mickey sold the Annex, however, he signed a non-compete agreement stating that he couldn't open another

coffee shop or bar below 14th Street. That's when he found another space located on Park Avenue South and 17th Street, a former pharmacy-turned-restaurant called the Southern.

Now he needed to name the place Mickey knew he wanted to serve steak. When he mentioned this to his friend, Joel Oppenheimer, Joel said when he thought of steak he thought of Kansas City because many of the great steakhouses served Kansas City beef. He chose the name Max because he said, "Wouldn't you eat at a place called Max's?" So in December of 1965, Max's Kansas City was born. Mickey also believed it would be cool to serve something at the bar for free, but not peanuts or pretzels. He offered chickpeas.

Max's was a two-floor restaurant and bar that was divided into the front room, the back room, the pack and the upstairs.

The front room was somewhat male oriented with many painters, poets, sculptors and artists hanging out there. Mickey did something very cool; he issued "Max's Charge Cards" to artists in exchange for artwork. It gave the artists a place to hang and schmooze art dealers and critics in style, even though they didn't have any cash.

In the back room, Andy Warhol frequently held court, and it was more

Lobby of the Gramercy Hotel

The Fillmore New York at Irving Plaza, 2008

female friendly—including drag queens. The producers of the film *Midnight Cowboy* actually recruited a bunch of extras for the movie from the back room.

The pack was situated between the front and back rooms. It was full of Max's regular celebrities like John and Yoko, Jagger, former New York City mayor Ed Koch, model Twiggy and from the fashion world, Halston and Betsy Johnson.

Upstairs was where the bands played Thursday through Sunday to a capacity of 125 people. the Velvet Underground, Television, Talking Heads, Blondie, Devo, Sid Vicious, the Heartbreakers, Alice Cooper, the New York Dolls, Iggy Pop, Waylon Jennings, Country Joe, Billy Joel, Bonnie Raitt, and Bruce Springsteen (who once opened here for Bob Marley!) played upstairs. Aerosmith also played at Max's, and the first time Columbia label-head Clive Davis saw them he signed them to a contract. Debbie Harry was a waitress at Max's before Blondie took off.

If you decided to dine, steak and lobster were the house specialties. A club steak would set you back $6.95, and a Maine lobster was $6.50. Or you could get surf and turf—what Max's called the "ship n' shore" special, one lobster tail and one small club steak for $8.50. A bottle of wine ran $3.00–$5.00, and if you wanted Max's house wine it was 90¢ a carafe. The most expensive champagne on the menu was Taittinger Brut N.V., which cost $12.00.

On New Year's Eve 1981, Max's Kansas City closed its doors for good.

ANDY WARHOL/FACTORY
Final Location
158 Madison Avenue @ 32nd Street

A former Con Edison building, Warhol moved the Factory here to its final location on December 3, 1984. This location was huge and had three separate entrances. Warhol decided to make use of the space by placing the Factory in one wing, *Interview* magazine in another and the third wing Warhol decided to rent out. It cost Warhol over $2 million to renovate the location. Warhol loved the space not only because of all the possibilities but because he could store an abundance of his paintings here. Andy Warhol passed away on February 22, 1987.

SEA OF CLOUDS
5 East 16th Street, 5th Floor

The Heartbreakers and the Ramones played a New Year's Eve show here. I was billed as a *New Year's Eve Champagne Party* with the Heartbreakers, the Ramones and DJ Wayne County.

KISS
Rehearsal Loft, 10 East 23rd Street

This was a fourth-floor rehearsal and audition loft for Kiss during the early '70s. It was also here that Paul Daniel Frehley, a.k.a. Ace, auditioned for the band. His friend Bob McAdams spotted an ad for a guitarist in *The Village Voice*. During the audition Ace showed up wearing one red sneaker and one orange sneaker. Three weeks after the audition, Ace was Kiss' lead guitarist.

GRAMERCY PARK HOTEL
2 Lexington Avenue

This 16-story hotel was built in 1925 and it's now one of the city's finest hotels. It has two bars that were voted best hotel bars in the city. The Rose and Jade bars are both edgy and eclectic. The private roof club and garden is an oasis 16 stories above Gramercy Park. This hotel remains a favorite among musicians. Madonna, the Clash and David

Warhol's Union Square Factory, 2008

ANDY WARHOL/FACTORY
Third Location
860 Broadway @ 17th Street

In September of 1974, the Factory moved to its third location. One of the cool things about this location is that it had a rear entrance and a second staircase. Warhol loved it and claimed that if he didn't want to be bothered by a "prima donna," he could exist without anyone knowing of his whereabouts. It was also at this Factory that Warhol began to hire foreign receptionists. Warhol did this to discourage people and fans from hanging out. A number of celebrities stopped calling and bothering Warhol after repeatedly spelling their name four, five or six times for the receptionist. What a great way to piss people off.

owie were former guests. the Grateful Dead actually played a gig on the roof in the '60s. Punk-rock icon Debbie Harry used to live here, and scenes from the movie *Almost Famous* starring Kate Hudson were shot here. Also, in 1929, movie legend Humphrey Bogart married his first wife Helen Menken at the Gramercy Hotel. In 2003, former Studio 54 owner Ian Schrager bought the hotel. The lobby houses exhibits by great 20th-century artists like Andy Warhol, Keith Haring and Jean-Michel Basquiat.

GRAMERCY ARTS THEATER
38 East 27th Street

This 140-seat theater played host to Andy Warhol's screening of the movie *Kiss* in the fall of 1963. The Gramercy Art Theater at one time was hailed as an underground mecca for creativity.

IRVING PLAZA/CLUB 57/ THE FILLMORE NEW YORK AT IRVING PLAZA
17 Irving Place

Upon entering Irving Plaza you need to ascend a flight of stairs to get to the concert hall. Once in the hall you are quickly reminded that you may be in a very big loft. Prior to becoming one of the world's premier concert halls, Irving Plaza was a Polish-American meeting hall, a cabaret hall, a swing dance hall and an Off-Broadway theater. It was also know as Club 57. Capacity for shows is about 1,000 people. In addition to the bar opposite the stage, there is also an upstairs bar and a small horseshoe balcony that is usually reserved for VIPs. The very first gig that Sonic Youth played under that name was here at Club 57. Some of the past performers at Irving Plaza include U2, Bob Dylan, Eric Clapton, Patti Smith, Marilyn Manson, Johnny Cash, Henry Rollins, Primus, Joe Strummer, Iggy Pop, Jon Spencer and the Hives. Concert Promoter Live Nation took over in 2007, and in April of that year renamed the club The Fillmore New York at Irving Plaza.

RCA VICTOR STUDIO
55 Lexington Avenue

Originally built in 1907 as a seven-story stable for horses, this became the site of the RCA Studios years later. It was here on July 2, 1956, that Elvis Presley recorded the singles "Don't Be Cruel" and "Hound Dog." It's now the site of Baruch College Business School.

PAUL KRASSNER
Apartment, 318 East 18th Street

Paul Krassner was the founder and editor of the *The Realist*, a magazine founded in 1958 that focused on radical humor and shattered many barriers. Krassner is also one of the founding members of the "Yippies." He lived here in 1966.

Kiss loft on East 23rd Street

35th st.

Often referred to as Midtown Manhattan, this neighborhood, along with Downtown and Uptown, covers Manhattan's three subdivisions. Geographically it reaches from 31st Street to 59th Street and from 3rd Avenue to 9th Avenue. The area is approximately two miles. It's also home to some of New York's most famous landmarks, such as Rockefeller Center, the Chrysler Building, Radio City Music Hall, Carnegie Hall, Times Square, the Theater District, United Nations headquarters, Grand Central Terminal, Museum of Modern Art and the Waldorf-Astoria Hotel. Midtown Manhattan is considered the busiest commercial district in the United States, and contains the majority of skyscrapers in New York City. Over one million people work in the Midtown area.

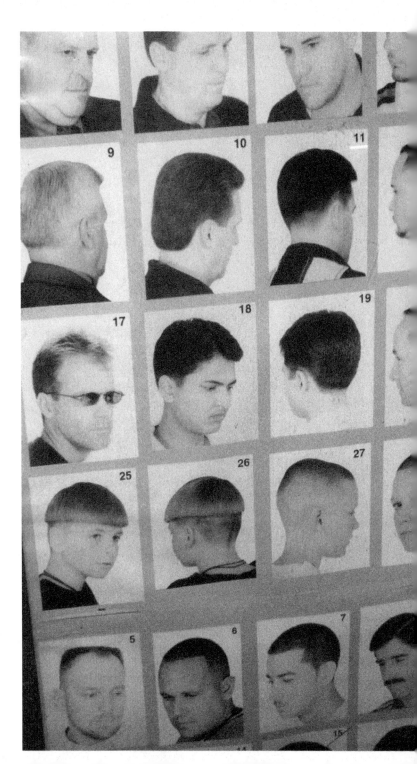

ROSELAND BALLROOM
239 West 52nd Street

Roseland was once a grand ballroom that catered to the swing kids of yesteryear. Now, Roseland Ballroom is primarily a standing-only concert hall, which holds 3,200 people downstairs and another 300 in the balcony. Some incredible shows have taken place here, including the Rolling Stones' *Licks 2002–2003 World Tour*, Bob Dylan, the White Stripes, Soundgarden, Smashing Pumpkins and Rancid.

On July 23, 1993, during the then-annual *New Music Seminar* music industry event, Nirvana took the stage. It was just hours before Nirvana was to perform when it was allegedly reported that Kurt Cobain suffered a drug overdose in his hotel room. Other events have also taken place here, most notably the annual New York City Tattoo Convention.

DIPLOMAT HOTEL
108 West 43rd Street

The Diplomat Hotel was a rather seedy hotel located in Times Square near a number of porn theaters. The hotel had a room called "The Palm Room" that would host rock shows. On May 29, 1972, the New York Dolls played one of their earliest New York gigs here. On July 13, 1973, Kiss performed at The Palm Room. At this point in their career they had played about a dozen shows. Kiss opened for the Brats that night. In the crowd was Neil Bogart of Casablanca Records, with whom they discussed a recording deal. It was also at the Diplomat in room 1015 that Abbie Hoffman was busted for cocaine, which for him was the beginning of years of legal problems.

MTV STUDIOS
1515 Broadway

This is the former site of the Astor Hotel, which was built in 1904. During its heyday, it had some pretty famous guests, including Carmen Miranda, Jimmy Durante and Will Rogers. It's now the U.S. headquarters of MTV. MTV went on the air August 1, 1981, and the very first video they aired was "Video Killed the Radio Star" by the Buggles. The second video was Pat Benatar's "You Better Run." Hey, what the hell happened to the videos?

TAFT HOTEL
Stones Video
7th Avenue @ 50th Street

Built in 1926, the Taft Hotel was on the northern fringe of Times Square.

In 1981, the Rolling Stones released *Tattoo You*. The album contained such hits as "Start Me Up," "Hang Fire," "Waiting on a Friend," and "Neighbors." Michael Lindsay-Hogg directed the videos for all four of those songs. "Neighbors" was filmed at the Taft. The concept of the video was that Mick Jagger had some noisy "neighbors" on either side of his hotel/apartment room. Jagger is then seen hanging out the window of the Taft

Roseland Ballroom, 2002

shouting the chorus "Neighbors, neighbors, neighbors."

When William Burroughs arrived in New York in 1939, he stayed at the Taft. He was evicted from the hotel when a house detective found him in bed naked with another man.

MANNY'S MUSIC
156 West 48th Street

Manny's opened for business at this Times Square location in 1935. Some of the greatest bands and musicians in the world have shopped here. Nirvana, U2, Eric Clapton, the Who, Jimi Hendrix and the Beatles have all been to Manny's. On July 11, 1965, Jimi Hendrix dropped by and spent nearly $2,000 on an Epiphone Casino, a Les Paul and an Echoplex. On January 23, 1974, Johnny and Dee Dee Ramone made the trek to Manny's from Queens, where Johnny bought his very first guitar, a $50.00 Mosrite. Manny's closed in the spring of 2009 due to the continued expansion of Rockefeller Center.

RUDY'S MUSIC STOP
169 West 48th Street

Opened in 1978 on Music Row, Rudy Pensa turned his passion into a dream with this guitar shop. One of the earliest Pensa-built guitars was the "R Custom." In 1985, he and Dire Straits frontman Mark Knopfler collaborated on plans for the "Pensa MK." Rudy is considered the Latino equivalent of Les Paul. Many rock stars have played his guitars, including Eric Clapton, Joe Perry, Carlos Santana and Lou Reed.

HOTEL NAVARRO
112 Central Park South

During the summer of 1969, about one month before *Woodstock*, Jimi Hendrix stayed here. During his time here he wrote the lyrics to "Ball and Chain" and "Let It Grow." The location is now the Ritz-Carlton.

ATLANTIC RECORDS
West 56th Street between
6th Avenue and Broadway

Atlantic Records was founded in September of 1947 by 24-year-old Ahmet Ertegun and his partner Herb Abramson

MTV Studios, 2007

Beatlemania conquered the Ed Sullivan Theater in 1964

The very first office of Atlantic Records was in the Jefferson Hotel on West 56th Street between 6th and Broadway. The label has been home to thousands of great musicians, including Led Zeppelin, Ray Charles, Cream, Professor Longhair and the Rolling Stones.

THE SUPPER CLUB
240 West 47th Street

The Supper Club is an art deco ballroom located in the heart of New York City's Theater District. It can accommodate up to 1,000 people and has a wonderful state-of-the art sound system. Bob Dylan performed four shows over two nights at the famed Supper Club on November 16 and 17, 1993. They distributed 200 free tickets to the fans and those shows have become quite legendary among Dylan fans, and critics. A couple of the songs Dylan played that night were "Queen Jane Approximately" and "One Too Many Mornings." On Halloween night, October 31, 2002, The Foo Fighters played here as part of their *One by One* tour.

BOND INTERNATIONAL CASINO
1526 Broadway @ 45th Street

This former department store and disco is where the Clash made history in May and June of 1981 when they played an unprecedented 17 shows. Capacity of Bond International Casino was listed at 1,800—however, the promoters were selling twice as many tickets per show. On Saturday, May 30th the New York City Fire Department cancelled the show, making the 3,640 fans attending fairly pissed off. The Clash cited greed by the promoters for overbooking and agreed to play additional dates. The Department of Buildings was threatening to close the club, thus canceling all the shows. But the club complied with building inspectors, installed some fire exit signs and made some other alterations. They were allowed to reopen, provided they didn't exceed the 1,800-person capacity. The Clash played more shows to accommodate those that had bought the "oversold" tickets. The June 9th show has often been bootlegged. The night opened with "London Calling."

ED SULLIVAN THEATER
1697 Broadway @ 53rd Street

Arthur Hammerstein built this Neo-Gothic style venue between the years 1925–1927. He named it Hammerstein's Theater. It was later renamed the Manhattan Theater and the Billy Rose Music Hall. In 1936, CBS acquired the lease and named it Radio Theater 3, followed by CBS Radio Playhouse. In 1950, it was converted to a TV studio and renamed CBS-Studio 50. In 1967, it was renamed the Ed Sullivan Theater for CBS variety-show host Ed Sullivan.

It was at CBS Studio 50, on February 9, 1964, at 8:00 pm that the U.S. viewing public got its first taste of Beatlemania. Nearly 50,000 people requested a ticket for that night, but capacity was only 728.

Manny's guitar store

Over 24 million households were tuned in that night to the *Ed Sullivan Show* with an estimated 73 million viewers. It was noted that during the one-hour show no crimes were reported in the U.S. The Beatles played five songs—"All My Loving," "Til There Was You," "She Loves You," "I Saw Her Standing There," and "I Want to Hold Your Hand."

The Beatles were paid $3,000 for the performance that night. Other performers on the show included Frank Goshin (later the Riddler on the *Batman* TV series), singer Tessie O'Shea, magician Fred Kaps (who had the misfortune of following the Beatles), comedian McCall and Brill, acrobats Wells and Four Fays and kids from the Broadway cast of *Oliver*. One of the kids was future Monkee Davey Jones. After the monumental show, DJ Murray the K took everyone except a sick George Harrison to the Playboy Club on 59th Street. After that the Beatles headed to the Peppermint Lounge, where they partied until 4:00 am.

On May 12, 1963, Bob Dylan was invited to play the *Ed Sullivan Show*. Dylan chose to perform "Talking John Birch Society Blues." Sullivan was somewhat reluctant to permit Dylan to sing that number because of its content and message. He later agreed, only to have the show's editor of programming deny Dylan permission. Dylan refused to give in and change the song and walked out. Dylan would never appear on the *Ed Sullivan Show*.

On October 25, 1964, the Rolling Stones made their first apearance on the *Ed Sullivan Show*. The Stones performed two songs: "Time Is on My Side" and "Around and Around." On January 15, 1967, the Stones once again performed on the show, and Sullivan, thinking the words "Let's spend the

The newly named U2 Way, 2009

night together" were a bit risqué, had the Stones change the words to "Let's spend some time together". They obliged. I guess the Stones don't piss anywhere!

On September 17, 1967, the Doors were facing the same request from Sullivan. On the Doors' current mega hit, "Light My Fire," Sullivan wanted singer Jim Morrison to change the words "Girl, we couldn't get much higher," implying the word "higher" was not suitable for his audience. However, when the Doors were performing the song live, Morrison sang "Girl, we couldn't get much higher." Well, Sullivan freaked out and said to Morrison, "You will never play the *Ed Sullivan Show* again." Morrison said, "Who cares, I just did." Now that's fucking rock n' roll!

Today, the *Late Show with David Letterman* tapes in CBS Studio 50, the same studio that gave birth to Beatlemania.

U2 WAY
53rd Street @ Broadway

Who said the streets have no name? In March of 2009 Mayor Bloomberg honored the Irish rockers with a street named after them. The band was in New York to

launch their new album *No Line On the Horizon* and to be the musical guest all week on the *Late Show with David Letterman*. They finished out the week by performing a small gig at Fordham University in the Bronx.

NBC STUDIOS
30 Rockefeller Center

Rockefeller Center is comprised of 11 acres of land and 19 commercial buildings from 49th Street to 52nd Street and from 5th Avenue to 7th Avenue. Thirty Rockefeller Center is the tallest, and probably the most widely known building, among the bunch. It's the home of the television show *Saturday Night Live*, which debuted on October 11, 1975, in studio 8H. So many great musicians have been the musical guests on *SNL*, including Bruce Springsteen, Nirvana, Foo Fighters, Pearl Jam, Chuck Berry, Talking Heads, Blondie, Bob Dylan, David Bowie, Madonna, the White Stripes and the Rolling Stones. On October 7, 1978, the Stones performed three songs from their recently released *Some Girls* album: "Beast of Burden," "Shattered" and "Respectable."

Originally all the Stones were to be in a skit featuring John Belushi as a bouncer in charge of the backstage guest list at a Stones show. During the proposed skit, Belushi was talking to Keith Richards

Carnegie Hall

Rollins and Ian MacKay drove from Washington D.C. to New York to see Black Flag at the Peppermint Lounge. In the early '80s, the club moved to its second and last location at 100 5th Avenue. The Peppermint Lounge lasted through the '80s before closing for good.

about doing a show at the "Afrodome" in Rhodesia (now Zimbabwe) with Lou Rawls. When Belushi asked if he was going to be able to make the show, Keith responded by saying "I can't, every February I go to Switzerland to get my blood changed." While watching the 7:30 pm dress rehearsal, the censors deemed the skit too off color, so the skit never made it to live television.

PEPPERMINT LOUNGE
128 West 45th Street

This was the original location of the Peppermint Lounge, one of the most famous clubs in New York City. The "Twist" was a dance craze that got its start here in 1955 when singer Hank Ballard saw kids doing the dance and wrote the song. But it wasn't until 1960, when Chubby Checker debuted the song and dance on the Dick Clark show *American Bandstand*, that America took notice.

The Beatles were taken to the Peppermint Lounge after their first performance on the *Ed Sullivan Show*. Some hardcore shows also took place here. In the spring of 1981, Henry

STEVE PAUL
The Scene, 301 West 46th Street

Imagine a Midtown club in the Theater District that had a surreal decadence and hosted some of rock's greatest performers, and you have Steve Paul's The Scene. Those that graced the stage here include the Velvet Underground, Traffic, Pink Floyd, Jeff Beck, Chambers Brothers, Howlin' Wolf and Jimi Hendrix. the Doors were a favorite of The Scene, and they were the biggest draw in the club's history. Led Zeppelin loved to hang out at The Scene, as did the post-party Andy Warhol Factory crowd, which turned The Scene into a decadent after-hours club. Rumor has it that the club housed and fed singer Tiny Tim for three years.

Entrance to The Scene

ANDY WARHOL
Silver Factory
231 East 47th Street

Andy Warhol's Factory had four different locations, but this was the very first, and it was called the "Silver Factory." Warhol's friend, Billy Name, who covered just about everything in tin foil and silver paint, decorated the space. Warhol named the place the "Factory" because he said it was a place that would manufacture people, ideas, concepts, film and art. Warhol rented the fifth-floor space in January of 1964. Although everyone referred to it as the Factory, those that actually worked here simply called it "the office."

In 1963, Andy Warhol filmed his first movie called *Sleep*. His movies were very stark and voyeuristic. Other Warhol films made during the early '60s were *Eat*, *Empire*, *Haircut*, *Bitch*, *Handjob*, *Drink* and *Blowjob*. Many of those movies were conceived here. Those that hung out at the Factory included the Velvet Underground, who often rehearsed here, Mick Jagger, Ultra Violet, Candy Darling, Holly Woodlawn, Billy Name, Brian Jones, Dennis Hopper and many others.

The very first pieces of art Warhol created at the Silver Factory were the "Food Boxes," namely those of Heinz Tomato Ketchup, Brillo, Kellogg's Corn Flakes and Mott's Apple Sauce. Many of Warhol's most famous paintings were done here, including "Cows" and "Flowers." At the end of 1967, the building's landlord notified Warhol that it was going to be torn down. Warhol relocated the Factory to 33 Union Square West.

LED ZEPPELIN
Drake Hotel, 440 Park Avenue

Led Zeppelin's 1973 North American Tour began on May 4th at Fulton County Stadium in Atlanta, Georgia, and ended on July 29th at Madison Square Garden in New York City. The tour began just after the release of Zep's fifth album *Houses of the Holy*. The three dates at Madison Square Garden were filmed for the theatrical release of *The Song Remains the Same*. The film not only showed the band ripping it up on stage, but also documented the theft of $203,000 from the Drake Hotel safe deposit box prior to the July 29th show. The stolen cash was earnings from the previous two nights at the Garden. The money was never recovered and the thieves never caught.

CARNEGIE HALL
154 West 57th Street

Icons or landmarks define most cities, and Carnegie Hall is that for New York.

Paramount Theater, 2008

Rudy's Music Stop, 2008

On February 12, 1964 three days after they played the *Ed Sullivan Show*, the Beatles played the Isaac Stern Auditorium. Tickets were priced from $3.00 for the balcony to $5.50 for the boxes. The band was returning to New York after their very first U.S. concert in Washington D.C. February 12th happened to be Lincoln's Birthday and a National Holiday, so the crowd that met the Beatles at Penn Station swelled to over 10,000. They played two, 34-minute shows that night at 7:45 and 11:15 pm.

It is the embodiment of performance excellence. Built in 1890, and founded and paid for by Andrew Carnegie, it was intended to be the home of the Oratorio Society of New York and the New York Symphony Society, for which Andrew Carnegie served as a board member. Peter Tchaikovsky was the first conductor to perform on opening night on May 5, 1891.

Carnegie Hall is comprised of three stages. The Isaac Stern Auditorium has seating for 2,804. The mid-size room is Zakel Hall, which seats 599, and the smallest is Weill Hall, formerly known as Chapter Hall, seating 268 patrons.

On Saturday November 8, 1961, at 8:40 pm, Bob Dylan's first "solo concert" was held at Chapter Hall. All seats were priced at $2.00, and 53 people attended the show—mostly Dylan's acquaintances who got in for free. Dylan played the following songs: "In the Pines" by Leadbelly, "Young but Daily Growin'," "Pretty Peggy O," "Black Girl In the Pines," "Gospel Plow," "1913 Massacre," "Blackwater Blues," "Fixin' to Die" and "This Land is Your Land."

On June 20, 1964, the Rolling Stones played their first concert in New York City, playing two shows at Carnegie Hall—one in the afternoon and one in the evening. The Stones opened the shows with "Not Fade Away" and closed with "I'm Alright." Bobby Goldsboro and Jay and the Americans were also on the bill, and it was Jay and the Americans that closed the show in order to "cool the fans down." That night was also the first time the Stones met Bob Dylan and got to hang out with the hip New York scene.

On October 17, 1969, Led Zeppelin played two shows at Carnegie Hall, and on November 23, 1971, the Doors, minus Jim Morrison, played Carnegie Hall. Carnegie Hall was renovated in 1986.

HENRY HUDSON HOTEL
353 West 57th Street

On October 31, 1966, the Doors arrived in New York City for the first time and checked into the Henry Hudson Hotel. That night they attended a Halween party at Ondines on the Upper East Side. It was also at this hotel that Leonard Cohen wrote the song "Lady Midnight."

PARAMOUNT THEATER
1501 Broadway
Times Square

Studio 54, 2008

The Paramount Theater was opened in 1926 by Paramount Pictures and served as the company's headquarters. The 3,600-seat theater served as Paramount's venue to screen new films. On September 20, 1964, the Beatles performed here—their only benefit concert during their three U.S. tours. The show benefited the United Cerebral Palsey and the Retarded Infants Services charities. Tickets were $1.50 for the balcony and $2.50 for the orchestra. The show was attended by a full house of 3,682 people, and it concluded the Beatles' 1964 American tour. In 1965, the theater was gutted and turned into office and retail space, and today New York City's Hard Rock Cafe occupies the ground floor.

BIRDLAND
Original Location
1678 Broadway @ 53rd Street

This was the original location of Birdland and named by owners Morris and Irving Levy after jazz great Charlie Parker. The basement club opened in 1949. Charlie Parker was usually the headliner, but the club also hosted Miles Davis, John Coltrane, Thelonious Monk and countless others. The 400-seat venue also attracted its share of celebrities, like Marilyn Monroe, boxer Joe Louis and Jack Kerouac. The original club closed in 1965 due to increasing rents, but in 1986 it reopened in Harlem at 2745 Broadway at 106th Street. Its current location is at 315 West 44th Street in Midtown.

STUDIO 54
254 West 54th Street

This building was once home to the Gallo Opera House, the New Yorker Theater, CBS Studio's and many other types of business. On April 26, 1977, it became known as Studio 54.

Opened by Steve Rubell and silent partner Ian Schrager, it became the destination for the jet-set crowd. Andy Warhol, Mick Jagger, Calvin Klein, Elton John, Truman Capote, Jackie Onassis and others would party the night away at Studio 54. The club was known for its hedonism and sexual encounters, and drug use was fairly rampant. Tax evasion and changing tastes brought the club down, and when it closed for the first time in 1980, it was reported that law enforcement found money and cocaine hidden in the walls. It reopened briefly, and then closed its doors in March of 1986.

From 1989 to early 1993 it became the second incarnation of the Ritz, which hosted some great rock shows. It's now called Cabaret at Studio 54. If you're in Las Vegas, check out the 22,000 square foot Studio 54 at the MGM Grand.

DEBBIE HARRY
Playboy Club, 5 East 59th Street

Before Blondie exploded out of CBGB, Debbie Harry was a Playboy Bunny at this club, from 1968–1973. During this era, the Playboy Club was a very up-scale sophisticated business club that had members. Dinner was served and men wore suits and ties. The club ended up closing because of dwindling business and as a result

of other upscale gentleman clubs. Th three flagship Bunny Clubs in Chicag Los Angeles, and this one in Ne York City, closed on June 1, 198

WALDORF-ASTORIA
301 Park Avenue

The Waldorf-Astoria Hotel is a lan mark art-deco building on Manhattar East Side. It opened at this location c October 1, 1931, and at the time wa the world's largest and tallest hotel. Th previous location was the eventual sit of the Empire State Building.

The Waldorf-Astoria was on of the first hotels to com bine a rich elegance, an abur dance of amenities and quali service. It was the first hotel to intrc duce room service. It also house three, five-star generals. The Empir Room located in the hotel was a pre mier club in New York City and helpe advance the careers of Frank Sinatra an Diana Ross. So it's kind of a place tha

Grand Central Terminal

The Doors, Strange Days

needed an injection of rock n' roll to overcome the stuffiness.

On Halloween, 1973, the New York Dolls performed at the Waldorf-Astoria. They rocked the house, but certainly the highlight of the evening was a costume competition with first prize being a night on the town with the Dolls and a weekend for two at a motel near Newark Airport in New Jersey. During the 1987 Grammy awards, things became so dull that Frank Zappa and the Mothers decided to spice things up a bit. During a performance by Woody Herman's jazz band, Zappa and the Mothers walked on stage in some freaky outfits. They proceeded to dismember toy dolls and hand the limbs to the suits in the front row. Rock n' roll had come to the Waldorf!

THE DOORS
Strange Days Album Cover
152–156 East 36th Street
Sniffen Court

Sniffen Court, in Murray Hill, consisted of 10 brick stables constructed in the 1850s. The 1967 album *Strange Days*

was one of the Doors' greatest, featuring songs like "When the Music's Over," "Love Me Two Times," "Moonlight Drive" and "People are Strange." The album cover was shot on this side street called Sniffen Court in Murray Hill. It featured an assortment of circus-and-sideshow type characters, and there was a poster of the Doors on one of the buildings.

GRAND CENTRAL TERMINAL
Park Avenue @ 42nd Street

Grand Central Terminal opened for business on February 2, 1913. Grand Central Terminal is the busiest train station in the country and houses many shops and restaurants. The main concourse is 120-feet wide, 375-feet long and a whopping 125-feet high. In 1995, Carly Simon performed live in Grand Central Terminal for a one-time-only concert. Rolling Stone Mick Jagger joined her on her hit song "You're So Vain."

On July 11, 1989, the Rolling Stones rolled into Grand Central Terminal on a train to announce plans for their upcom-

The evening the Rolling Stones played Radio City in 2006

ing *Steel Wheels* world tour and their first new album in seven years. The station was sweltering hot, but more than 500 press people showed up to find out more about this tour and the new album. Mick Jagger proceeded to play a few of the bands' new songs on a portable boombox.

RAMONES
53rd & 3rd

53rd and 3rd in Manhattan was a notorious male-prostitution spot in New York City. The Ramones second single was "53rd & 3rd," and allegedly Dee Dee Ramone hustled at this corner to help pay for his drug habit. The corner is now home to one of New York's many skyscrapers, the Citigroup Center.

ONDINES
308 East 59th Street @ 3rd Avenue

Ondines was a small basement club that opened in 1965, and it eventually became a hangout for the Warhol Factory crowd. On November 1, 1966, the Doors gave their very first New York City performance at Ondines, having

The Plaza

been booked on reputation alone as Los Angeles's hippest new band. The Doors played for the entire month of November (except Thanksgiving, November 24th), playing five sets a night while spending their days working on their debut album. The owners had a policy of booking Los Angeles. bands. Buffalo Springfield played here six nights a week for three consecutive weeks for union scale.

NEW YORK PRESBYTERIAN HOSPITAL
25 East 68th Street

Andy Warhol checked himself into Baker Pavilion at New York Presbyterian Hospital on February 21, 1987. Andy was checked in under the name Bob Roberts and given room 1204. Warhol was in for a routine gall-bladder operation but died early in the morning on February 22, 1987, of an apparent heart attack.

METROPOLITAN OPERA HOUSE
Broadway @ 65th Street
Lincoln Center

In 1966, the Metropolitan Opera House landed at its current home at Lincoln Center. The Met's first home was on Broadway between 39th and 40th streets. Roughly 3,600 seats are split among six different sections. In June of 1970, the Who performed their rock opera *Tommy* for two consecutive nights. It was the very first time a rock band was permitted to perform at the Met. The Metropolitan Opera House was built in the '60s, replacing an old tenement building where *West Side Story* was filmed.

UNGANOS NIGHT CLUB
210 West 70th Street

In the '60s and '70s, most of the rock clubs were Downtown. So who would have thought that an Uptown club would have such a cool scene? Unganos on West 70th Street booked the Allman Brothers Band for their New York City debut. Also making their New York City debut was Detroit's own MC5. It was here that Iggy Pop scaled the ceiling during a performance by climbing along the pipes. Iggy has been one of rock's most exciting performers. Without a doubt he has earned the nickname "The Godfather of Punk."

In 1969, on the heels of their debut album, Led Zeppelin decided to hold a press conference here. In 1970, Jimi Hendrix, Buddy Miles and Elvin Bishop did an impromptu jam at the club. It was late at night when they walked into the nearly empty club. The few customers that were there began calling friends who called more friends. Before long the club was full, and Hendrix was laying down some tasty licks.

The fountain outside the Plaza

Uptown: 60th Street to 155th Street was largely considered at one time a "non-tourist" area of Manhattan. But since the early '70s things have changed, and now all of Manhattan is considered very "tourist friendly." New York City is comprised of five boroughs: Manhattan, Brooklyn, the Bronx, Queens and Staten Island. Uptown has the Upper West Side and Upper East Side, as well as Harlem, Spanish Harlem, Washington Heights, Inwood and Marble Hill. Landmarks include Central Park, the Apollo Theater, Grant's Tomb, the Cloisters, and many museums like the Guggenheim, Metropolitan Museum of Art and the American Museum of Natural History.

The Imagine mosaic in Strawberry Fields

STRAWBERRY
FIELDS

The entrance to Strawberry Fields

The Dakota

THE DAKOTA
West 72nd Street

The Dakota, on Manhattan's Upper West Side, was built during the years 1881–1984. The Dakota's architect, Henry Hardenbergh was also responsible for designing two other New York City landmark buildings, the Plaza and the Western Union Building. It was named the Dakota as a result of the building's location. The Dakota was being built Uptown, far away from other Downtown Manhattan neighborhoods. So city planners made the comment that because of its Uptown location, it might as well have been built in North Dakota.

Tenants of the building have included Paul Simon, Roberta Flack, Lauren Bacall, Leonard Bernstein, Judy Garland and John Lennon and Yoko Ono. The co-op board at the Dakota has also refused residency to quiet a few celebrities, including Gene Simmons and Billy Joel.

It was near 5:00 pm on December 8, 1980, that John and Yoko left their home at the Dakota to head to the Hit Factory on West 44th Street to transfer some of the newly released *Double Fantasy* recordings to singles. As they headed toward their waiting car, they were approached by a number of fans seeking autographs. One of those autograph seekers received an autograph from Lennon on the album *Double Fantasy*. John and Yoko spent about five hours at the studio and left for home at about 10:50 pm. Their car pulled up to the 72nd Street curb. Three witnesses saw a shadow just inside the arch. As John and Yoko walked by, a gunman said, "Mr. Lennon," then he went into a combat-style stance and fired four bullets into the body of the ex-Beatle. Lennon staggered to the concierge entrance and said, "I've been shot." Police officers say the gunman dropped the revolver and stood calmly by. On Lennon's person was J.D. Salinger's *The Catcher in the Rye* and cassette tapes containing 14 hours of Beatles music. Lennon was rushed to Roosevelt Hospital about 12-blocks away on the West Side, where he was pronounced dead at 11:15 pm. The world will forever miss John Lennon. On December 10, 1980, John Lennon was cremated. On December 14, 1980, at 2:00 pm, a 10-hour worldwide vigil took place. Yoko Ono and Paul McCartney, requested that the name of the killer never be repeated. I will not post his name, as he may benefit in some twisted way.

CAFE LA FORTUNA
69 West 71st Street
between Columbus Avenue and
Central Park West

A favorite cafe and hangout of John Lennon and Yoko Ono opened in 1976 and served tasty Italian sandwiches, coffees and pastries. A few times a week, John and Yoko would stop here to eat, or maybe just have an espresso or tea. Lennon would often write songs, poetry or just sketch. They had a favorite table, which was featured on the single cover-sleeve "Nobody Told Me." After Lennon's death, the owner, Vincent Urwand, gave Yoko the table and chairs

as a gift. There was plenty of Lenno memorabilia at the cafe, including som cool photos and letters from Yoko.

In the 2006 TV special *The Spirit of Joh Lennon*, British psychic Joe Power pa a visit to the cafe and used many the objects and pictures in an attemp to connect with Lennon's spirit. Due increasing rents the restaurant close February 24, 2008.

DIZZY GILLESPIE
Apartment, 2040 7th Avenue

In 1944, Dizzy Gillespie was mus director for Billy Eckstine's band. It wa during this era that both Dizzy and Bil resided in this building.

NEW YORK COLISEUM
Columbus Circle

Built in 1954, replacing the Majestic The ater, the New York Coliseum hosted trad shows, conventions and an occasiona concert. On November 14, 1993, Nir

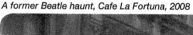

A former Beatle haunt, Cafe La Fortuna, 2008

ana played the 7,000-seat Coliseum, which sold out immediately. Nirvana opened the show with "Drain You," "Breed" and "Serve the Servants" and played for well over an hour. The New York Coliseum was demolished in 2000. It was replaced by the 55-story Time Warner Center.

TRAX
100 West 72nd Street

This small Upper West Side industry-showcase club hosted quite a few memorable nights. On September 27, 1977,

New York City's teddy-bear hospital, 2007

the Rolling Stones, along with Andy Warhol, held a launch party at Trax for their double LP, *Love You Live*.

HURRAH
36 West 62nd Street

A post-punk club in the '80s, this place certainly created it's own buzz Uptown. The Go Go's, the Waitresses, the Flesh-tones, Pylon and many others played here. The Young Marbles, a band that received much critical acclaim from Michael Stipe and Kurt Cobain, had a live show recorded at Hurrah. It's said to be the only visual performance ever record-ed by the band.

CHURCH OF ST. JOHN NEPOMUCENE
411 East 66th Street

Dee Dee Ramone wed Vera Boldis at this Upper East Side church in September 1978, one day before the Ramones were to leave on a month-long tour of Europe. Vera's parents were also married at this church, and Vera was bap-

tized here. About 50 people were invited. Joey Ramone and Tommy Ramone made it, but Johnny didn't. The reception afterwards took place in Queens, and Dee Dee said that they should hire the Dead Boys to play the reception. They decided upon a traditional wedding band that played the Beatles, disco and some wedding songs.

ANDY WARHOL
Final Residence, 57 East 66th Street

Andy Warhol lived here from 1974 until his death on February 22, 1987. He paid $310,000 for this brownstone located between Madison Avenue and Park Avenue. Andy kept many of his collectibles here, including cookie jars, Navajo blanket rugs and rare furniture.

BEACON THEATER
2124 Broadway @ 74th Street

The Beacon Theater opened in 1928 as a 2,800-seat vaudeville hall. When silent movies became known as "talkies" in the late '20s, the Beacon became a premier movie house. Nowadays, the Beacon Theater is a nationally registered "art-deco" landmark, and the interior is legally protected from any form of alteration. The Rolling Stones played two shows here in 2006—one show was the 60th birthday party for former U.S. President Bill Clinton. Martin Scorsese filmed both shows for the Rolling Stones movie *Shine A Light*.

The Allman Brothers Band play a legendary two-week residency every March, often featuring guest musicians like Peter Frampton, Dave Mason, Chris Robinson and Leslie West. Musicians love the theater because of its great acoustics, design and old-school charm. Patrons love it for the same reasons. The Beacon was closed in 2008 for a $16 million renovation and re-opened in February 2009 with a conce... by Paul Simon. Simon was joined at th... show by Art Garfunkel.

NEW YORK DOLL HOSPITAL
787 Lexington Avenue @ 61st Street

Where exactly would you get repaired priceless heirloom doll that lost a limb... To a hospital of course, the New Yor... Doll Hospital! Situated in a very unpre... tentious brownstone on the Upper Eas... Side, it's the only toy hospital in Ne... York City. Doll limbs, eyeballs, hand... toy feet and toy clothing surround fou... or five employees. In the early '70s whe... Johnny Thunders, Jerry Nolan and Da... vid Johansen were forming a band, ... was Sylvain Sylvain who worked acros... the street from the hospital and wa... intrigued by the name New York Do... Hospital. Suggesting it as a band nam... they became known as the Dolls of Ne... York. However it was Arthur Kane wh... wanted to call the group the New Yor... Dolls, citing the New York Yankees an... New York Giants as inspiration, but als... noting that the name sounded like ... '30s Broadway show. The hospital ha...

Conservatory Pond in Central Park

ad many celebrity customers
ver the years, and allegedly
ruce Springsteen brought his
d teddy bear in for repairs.

2009, owner Irving Chais
assed away at the age of 83.
he family decided to retire the
usiness in the spring of 2009.

HE PLAZA HOTEL
th Avenue @ Central Park
outh

ne Plaza is one of New York
ity's most celebrated hotels.
ne 19-story hotel first opened
r business on October 1, 1907.

Mad Hatter at Alice in Wonderland, Central Park

ne Plaza has been featured in many
ollywood productions including Hitch-
ock's *North by Northwest*, *The Great
iatsby*, *Barefoot in the Park* and many
thers. On February 7, 1964, Beatlema-
ia hit the Plaza. The Beatles checked
i and were given the 12th floor Presi-
ential Suite, rooms 1209–1216, which
ccupied the entire floor. Upon their ar-
val, there were over 100,000 pieces of
an mail awaiting them. There were so
nany fans waiting for the Beatles out-
ide the Plaza that the New York Police
Department assigned 100 mounted of-
cers to the hotel for the entire week-
nd. The Ronettes, DJ Murray the K
nd George Harrison's sister visited the
Beatles that first night. Their first official
J.S. press conference was held at the
Plaza, featuring some classic questions
and memorable answers such as, Q:
Are you going to get your haircut? A:
George: I had one yesterday.

During their last night in the Plaza on
February 12th, the Beatles enjoyed a
it of New York City nightlife. At about
4:30 am, they left to visit the Headliner
Club and then moved on to the Improvisational Coffee House in Greenwich Vil-
age. They returned to the Plaza about

7:00 am in order to catch a February
13th, 1:30 pm flight to Miami.

In 1969 the Plaza was designated as
a New York City landmark. In 2005 the
Plaza announced that some of the hotel
rooms would be converted into residential condos. Recently the Plaza sold one
of its penthouse condos for a record
$53.5 million.

COPACABANA
10 East 60th Street

The original location of the Copacabana was located in the basement of
Hotel Fourteen at 10 East 60th Street.
Often referred to as the most famous
nightclub in the world, the Copacabana
opened its doors in 1941. Many memorable movie scenes were shot here, including one from *Goodfellas*. The Copacabana moved its location to West 34th
Street but recently was forced to move
yet again due to more construction on
the West Side of Manhattan.

CENTRAL PARK
60th Street to 110th Street

Central Park, designed by landscape
architect Frederick Law Olmsted and
Calvert Vaux, was the very first land-

scaped park in the United States. It occupies a vast 843 acres. In the 1800s, wealthy merchants and landowners admired European parks in London and Paris and realized that if New York was to become the city they dreamed of, they would need to design an unbelievable park where families would gather for carriage rides and picnics. They also hoped the park would keep many men out of the saloons by having them do things with their family in the park.

Here are just a few of the park's offerings:

Wollman Rink
Central Park South

Nature Sanctuary
East 60th Street

Bowling and Croquet Greens

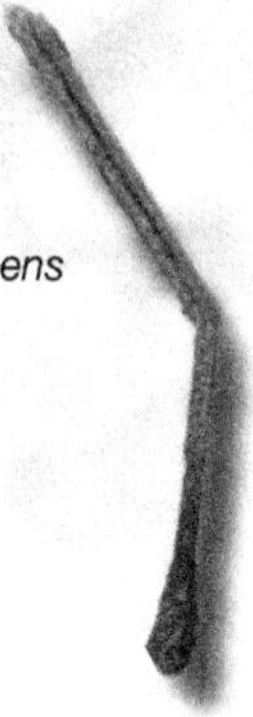

West 69th Street

Conservatory Garden
East 105th Street

Great Lawn
East 79th Street

Central Park Zoo

Lawn bowling in Central Park

East 64th Street
Tavern on the Green
West 66th Street

Boathouse Restaurant
East 74th Street

Alice in Wonderland
East 75th Street

Belvedere Castle
East 79th Street

Strawberry Fields
West 72nd Street

Shakespeare Garden
West 79th Street

Central Park Tennis Courts
West 96th Street

SUMMER STAGE PERFORMANCE
West 72nd Street

SUMMER STAGE

The City Parks Foundation each summer offers free concerts in the park Sometimes there is a cover charg depending on the act. Some past pe formers have included Curtis Mayfiel Lou Reed, Sonic Youth, Elvis Costell Annie Lennox, Jim Carroll, Richa

The original background for Electric Ladyland

Hell, Luscious Jackson, Black Crowes, Joan Jett, B-52s, Yeah Yeah Yeahs, the Strokes and Devo.

STRAWBERRY FIELDS

Soon after John Lennon's death, Yoko Ono asked the city if she could landscape a plot of land in Central Park in John's memory. Strawberry Fields consists of 2.5 acres for which Yoko paid $1 million to the Central Park Conservancy to landscape and maintain the grounds. The area was named Strawberry Fields after the Beatles' song "Strawberry Fields Forever." The area contains 150 different species of plants—which was one plant for each nation that contributed to the memorial. There is an "Imagine" mosaic and a monument in the park that reads, "Strawberry Fields, Imagine all the people living in peace."

- Landscape architect, Bruce Kelly, designed Strawberry Fields. Bruce was a principal member of the Central Park Conservancy's management and restoration team.

- The "Imagine" mosaic is a reproduction of a mosaic from Pompeii. It was created by Italian craftsman and was a gift from Naples, Italy.

- Strawberry Fields was dedicated by then-Mayor Ed Koch on October 9, 1985, John Lennon's birthday.

ALICE IN WONDERLAND

It was in August of 1968 that the Jimi Hendrix Experience hired Linda Eastman (later Linda McCartney) to photograph them as they were cavorting about the Alice in Wonderland statues for their upcoming album *Electric Ladyland*. The band was certainly having fun, but the photos were scrapped at the last moment in favor of 21 naked women who graced the album's cover. Those shots by Linda later made it into the inside cover of the album on their U.S. release.

BETHESDA FOUNTAIN

Blondie played a New Year's Eve show here, 1976–1977, for the New York City Department of Parks and Recreation of Central Park. The temperature was hov-

R.L. Burnside, Summer Stage, 2000

ering around 18° F during their perfor-mance and there were about six inches of slush on the ground. Blondie rocked however, and collected $1,500 for the gig—the most they ever were paid up to that point.

GREAT LAWN

The Great Lawn is the largest open space in Central Park, consisting of 55 acres and stretching from 79th Street to 85th Street. On September 19, 1981, Simon and Garfunkel held a free show on the Great Lawn, and 500,000 people showed up. It was their first appear-ance together since the 1972 George McGovern presidential campaign at Madison Square Garden. The show was documented and issued on CD, and later DVD, under the title *Simon and Garfunkel: The Concert in Central Park*. In 1983, Diana Ross tried her hand at a free concert, but it was postponed due to heavy rains. It was rescheduled for the next night, but a team of organized muggers disrupted it. Other musicians who have performed on the Great Lawn include Elton John and Luciano Pava-rotti. On July 12, 2008, Bon Jovi played a free concert to kick-off Major Leagu[e] Baseball's All-Star Week.

SHEEP MEADOW

This 15-acre grass mead-ow is a gathering spot for New Yorkers and tourists that want to relax and enjoy the sun. In 1970, rock promoter Bill Graham wanted to host a free concert for New York City in the Sheep Meadow, however, the city refused to al-low it because they were con-cerned about the enormous garbage cleanup. Bill Graham said h[e] would personally buy the city 160 ne[w] garbage cans for the event. The cit[y] agreed, and the show went on wit[h] Jefferson Airplane headlining. In 1985 the Jefferson Starship played a fre[e] show for 60,000 fans. This time the city charged the band $14,000 for the cleanup. On July 21, 1969, Led Zeppelin played a show in the Sheep Meadow. Take a look at Steeley Dan's *Pretzel Logic* album cover. It was shot in front of the Sheep Meadow using one of the park's many pretzel vendors as the main focus or the cover. In May of 1984, Chrissie Hynde of the Pretenders married Jim Kerr of Simple Minds in the park.

WOLLMAN SKATING RINK

Wollman Skating Rink was the host for long-running concert series called *The Outdoor Concert Series at Wollman Skating Rink*. Originally sponsored by Schaeffer Beer in the '70s, the concert series ended in the early '80s. On August 21, 1972, the Doors played Wollman Rink as part of the *Schaffer Beer Music Festival*. That was a little over 3 months after Jim Morrison passed away, and needless to say the show received horrible reviews. It was the last time the Doors played New York City. Other bands that played here include the Ramones and Todd Rundgren.

BILLIE HOLIDAY
Apartment, 108 West 139th Street

In 1932, 16-year-old Billie Holiday moved into this apartment building. Soon after she settled in, Billie got a gig singing at a club on West 133rd Street.

LENOX LOUNGE
288 Lenox Avenue @ 125th Street

Since 1939, many jazz legends have performed here. Miles Davis, John Coltrane and Billie Holiday are just a few. The Dave Matthews Band held a record-release party here on February 24, 2001.

VELVET UNDERGROUND
"Waiting for the Man"

The Velvet Underground's debut album, *The Velvet Underground & Nico*, is one of the most influential recordings of all time. One of the songs on that debut is "Waiting for the Man." The song follows a man making a heroin purchase while he's waiting with $26.00 in his hand on Lexington 1-2-5. Some people misunderstood the song and thought Lou Reed was talking about 125 Lexington Avenue. Not so. He was talking about a street corner in Harlem. However, at 125 Lexington Avenue, you can get some tasty curry.

APOLLO THEATER
253 West 125th Street

Built in 1914, and considered the mainstay for African American entertainment, the original name of the Apollo was the Hurtig and Seamons New Burlesque Theatre. African Americans were not permitted in the audience. In 1928, Bill Minsky transformed the burlesque house into the 125th Street Apollo Theater. The Apollo Theater finally opened its doors to African American customers in 1934.

The Apollo has launched the careers of many great artists such as Bessie Smith, Billie Holiday, James Brown, Diana Ross & the Supremes, Marvin Gaye, Stevie Wonder, Aretha Franklin and many more. On November 21, 1934 Ella Fitzgerald made her singing debut at the age of seventeen. The theater hit some rough times in the '60s and '70s, but it

Joan Jett, Summer Stage, 2000

was given landmark status in 1983 and was bought by the State of New York in 1991.

On December 28, 2006, the body of James Brown, who died a few days earlier, was displayed as a memorial to his legendary career. Only a handful of rock bands have played at the Apollo, including Buddy Holly in 1957, KORN in 1999, the Strokes in 2001, Björk in 2007 and Cat Power in 2009.

COTTON CLUB
Original Location
644 Lenox Avenue @ 142nd Street

This was the original site of the Cotton Club, which opened in 1923. It was originally owned by heavyweight boxer Jack Johnson and called Club De Lux. It was sold to gangster Owney Madden in 1923 and renamed the Cotton Club. The Cotton Club helped launch the careers of Duke Ellington, Cab Calloway and Bill "Bojangles" Robinson. Nine years after it opened, the Cotton Club moved to Broadway and 48th Street in Midtown due to race riots in Harlem. In 1940, the club closed its doors for good because of higher rents in Mid-   town. In 1978, the Cotton Club was reborn at 656 West 125th Street in Harlem, where it still thrives today.

ANDY WARHOL
Townhouse
1342 Lexington Avenue @ 89th Street

In 1959, Andy Warhol bought his first Manhattan property, a townhouse on the Upper East Side. It was on the northwest corner of Lexington and 89th Street. Andy lived here with his mother Julia.

JFK INTERNATIONAL AIRPORT
Jamaica, Queens

Consisting of 4,930 acres and located only 30 minutes from Midtown Manhat-

tan, JFK International Airport launched it first flight on July 1, 1948. At that time was dedicated as New York Internation Airport, but it was later renamed Idlewi Airport. Then on December 24, 1963, was renamed John F. Kennedy Airport.

Nearly 40 million passengers pas through JFK each year. But four passer gers arrived here that impacted the mu sic world forever. On February 7, 196 Pan American Yankee Clipper Flight 10 landed at JFK, bringing the Beatles t America. Over 3,000 screaming fan greeted the Beatles that afternoon. Ne York radio DJ Murray the K heavily pro moted the arrival of the Fab Four, an quickly dubbed himself the "Fifth Beatle. *The Saturday Evening Pos* noted, "Anyone listening to pop radio station in New Yor would hear a Beatles song ev ery four minutes." Less than tw months after they arrived, Th Beatles had the top five spots o the *Billboard* Top 100 singles char a feat that has never been equaled Beatlemania arrived! The airport wa also mentioned in U2's "Angel of Har lem." Many notable movie scenes wer shot at JFK, including scenes from *Goodfellas*, *Live and Let Die*, *Dog Da Afternoon* and *Catch Me If You Can*.

SHEA STADIUM
123–01 Roosevelt Avenue
Flushing, Queens

Construction of Shea Stadium began in the early '60s. The cost was about $25.5 million. The stadium was named after William Alfred Shea, who was very instrumental in bringing a National League baseball team back to New York City after the abandonment by the Brooklyn Dodgers and the New York Giants. The Stadium opened on April 17, 1964, with the New York Mets playing the

Joan Jett, Summer Stage, 2000

ittsburgh Pirates. The Mets lost 4–3, establishing the tortured temperature of ne franchise.

was on Sunday August 15, 1965, hat music history was made. It was the ery first show for the Beatles at Shea tadium. The show set an attendance ecord for a pop performance, drawing 5,600 fans. Concert promoter Sid Ber- stein presented the concert, and here's breakdown of that legendary show:

Tickets were priced at $5.65 ($5.00 plus various taxes).

Gross receipts for the concert totalled $304,000.

The Beatles' take-home pay was, $160,000 (57,000 pounds).

• Opening acts included Brenda Holloway, King Curtis Band, Cannibal and the Headhunters, Sounds Incorporated and the Young Rascals.

• Songs performed during the 35-minute show were "Twist and Shout", "She's a Woman," "I Feel Fine," "Dizzy Miss Lizzy," "Ticket to Ride," "Everybody's Trying to Be My Baby," "Can't Buy Me Love," "Baby's In Black," "Act Naturally," "Hard Day's Night," "Help," "I'm Down."

Other notables who played Shea Stadi- um include the Who and the Clash dou- ble bill, the Police, Simon and Garfunkel, Elton John and the Rolling Stones. The Stones played one of the last Shea Sta- dium shows in 1989 when they brought the *Steel Wheels* tour to New York City. In 1971, Grand Funk Railroad broke the Beatles' Shea Stadium record for ticket sales when they sold out two shows in less than three days. Shea Stadium also hosted the *Summer Festival For Peace* in 1970, featuring Jimi Hendrix, Creedence Clearwater Revival, Johnny Winter, Paul Simon, the James Gang and surprise-guest Janis Joplin. In July of 2008, Billy Joel performed the final two shows at Shea Stadium, and on the second night Paul McCartney joined him on stage. Shea Stadium was torn down after the 2008 baseball season, and the Mets have a new home next door called Citi Field.

Recognizing Warhol's last NYC residence

MOUNT ST. MARY'S CEMETERY
**172–00 Booth Memorial Avenue
Flushing, Queens**

Mount St. Mary's Cemetery is located in Flushing, Queens. It's the burial ground of former New York Doll and Heartbreaker members Johnny Thunders and Jerry Nolan. Johnny's grave is in Division 9, Row R, Grave 78.

Johnny Thunders was born John Anthony Genzale, Jr. on July 15, 1952. The name on the headstone reads Nicoletti,

Get your hot dogs here!

and in the bottom left-hand corner reads Johnny Thunders Genzale. Jer Nolan's grave is in Division 24, Row ♪ Grave 89. The headstone reads Jer Nolan, May 7, 1946–January 14, 199 Forever in our Hearts. Johnny Thunder died of a heroin overdose in New Orlear at the St. Peter House on April 23, 199

Jerry Nolan was suffering from bacte rial meningitis and bacterial pneumoni when he suffered a stroke and lapse into a coma, which he never recovere from. He passed awa while on life support. Th cemetery office is very hel ful and will provide a map requested.

COVENTRY
45th Street and Queens Boulevard, Flushing Queens

The Coventry was a club i Flushing, Queens where th band Kiss first got its star Kiss played at the Coven try January 28, 29 and 30 1973, and supposedly no many people showed up

r any of the three
shows. It's also ru-
mored that the name
Kiss was derived after
one of Flushing's ma-
jor streets, Kissena.

FOREST HILLS TENNIS STADIUM
Forest Hills, Queens

This was the original
building of the U.S.
Tennis Open. On
August 28 and 29,
1964, the Beatles

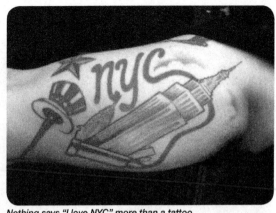
Nothing says "I love NYC" more than a tattoo

played here for a crowd of 16,000 each
night. The Beatles arrived by helicopter, and the concerts were barely au-
dible due to the screaming fans. Tickets
ranged from $1.95 to $7.50.
Tickets were being scalped
for as much as $50.00.
Also, on August 17, 1963,
Bob Dylan was introduced in
front of 15,000 fans as Joan
Baez' special guest. Dylan
performed "Only a Pawn
in Their Game" and "A
Hard Rain's A-Gonna
Fall" before being
joined by Joan Baez. They
sang "Troubled and I Don't Know
Why" and "Blowin' in the Wind."

RAMONES
FOREST HILLS HIGH SCHOOL
67–01 110th Street
Forest Hills, Queens

Located near Flushing Meadows Park,
this is the former high school of the Ramones', Joey, Dee Dee, Johnny and
Tommy. The high school was also featured in the 1995 movie *The Basketball
Diaries* starring Leonardo DiCaprio and
Mark Walhberg. Other notable alumni
are Paul Simon, Art Garfunkel and Leslie West.

ROCKAWAY BEACH
Queens

This is a neighborhood located on the
Rockaway Peninsula in Queens that
was once referred to as "The Irish Riv-
iera" because of its large Irish American population. It is also the largest
urban beach in the United States,
stretching for miles and miles. Co-
median George Carlin once said he
was conceived in Rockaway Beach
at Curley's Hotel. The Ramones
immortalized the area with their
1977 single "Rockaway Beach"
on their third album *Rocket to
Russia*. Dee Dee Ramone, who
said he loved going to the beach, wrote
the song. It was the Ramones' highest
charting single of their career in the U.S.,
making it to 66 on the *Billboard* Hot 100.

REGO PARK SUBWAY STATION
Rego Park, Queens

This subway station on the
Queens Boulevard line opened
in 1936, and believe it or not
there was a punk club lo-
cated in this station during the '80s. In 1985,
Das Damen and
Sonic Youth
played here.

The House That Ruth Built, 2008

DOWNING STADIUM/ICAHN STADIUM
Randall's Island

Downing Stadium was built in 1934 and in the '70s, served as the home to the New York Cosmos soccer club and the New York Stars of the WFL. It's also a popular concert venue, having hosted the *Tibetan Freedom Festival*, the *Warped Tour* and *Lollapalooza*. In 1936 over 40,000 people witnessed Jesse Owens participate in the Olympic Trials. Randall's Island is a 480-acre island located in the East River between Queens and Manhattan.

Menu at Nathan's, Coney Island, 2008

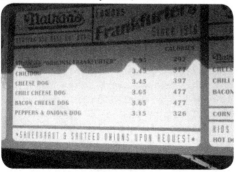

59TH STREET BRIDGE SONG
Queensboro Bridge

Completed in 1909, and connecting Queens with Manhattan, the Queensboro Bridge is also known as the 59th Street Bridge because the Manhattan side of the bridge is at 59th Street. The bridge became a part of pop culture in 1966 when Simon and Garfunkel recorded "The 59th Street Bridge Song (Feelin' Groovy)." The song appeared on the album *Parsley, Sage, Rosemary and Thyme*.

YANKEE STADIUM
161st Street and River Avenue Bronx

Yankee Stadium opened in 1923 and is considered by many sports fans to be as the most famous stadium in the world. The Stadium's nickname, "The House That Ruth Built," comes from the iconic legend Babe Ruth, whose years with the Yanks coincided with the opening of the stadium and many of their championships. Since 1923, Yankee Stadium has been host to 37 of 85 World Series, with the Yankees winning 26.

Music was never a big part of the Stadium's history, however, until the Isley Brothers performed the first Stadium show on June 21, 1969. The first "rock" show was by Billy Joel on June 22, 1990. U2 played two shows here during their *Zoo TV* tour in 1992, and Pink Floyd performed two sold out shows in support of the 1994 release *The Division Bell*. The last year for the House That Ruth Built was 2008. The Yankees currently play in the new Yankee Stadium, located directly across the street.

GAELIC PARK
240th Street and Broadway, Bronx

Gaelic Park is located in the Northeast section of the Bronx and has been a gathering spot for the Irish and Irish Americans for years. It contains a ball field and a dance hall. the Grateful Dead played here July 30, 1971, performing such songs as "Bertha," "Big Railroad Blues," 'Good Lovin'," "Truckin'" and "Uncle John's Band." Manhattan College and Howard Stein presented the show, and ticket prices were $4.00. Other bands to perform in Gaelic Park include the Wolftones and Black 47.

From 1920–1932, the Babe singlehandedly lifted baseball to new heights with his unlimited talent and unbridled love for the game. His enormous contributions to baseball and the Yankees made him the most celebrated athlete who ever lived.

Fans heading to the subway after a Yankee win

101 song

out new york city

I love lists and numbers.
So here are some of my favorite songs
about New York City.
They're in no particular order and I'm sure
I omitted some of your favorites.
But fuck it, here's mine:

1. Shattered — Rolling Stones
2. 53rd & 3rd — Ramones
3. New York — Sex Pistols
4. Angel of Harlem — U2
5. Broadway — The Clash
6. People Who Died — Jim Carroll
7. New York Groove — Ace Freeley
8. No Sleep Till Brooklyn — Beastie Boys
9. Talking New York — Bob Dylan
10. All My Friends in New York — NOFX
11. Central Park N' West — Ian Hunter
12. Christmas in Hollis — Run DMC
13. Avenue B — Iggy Pop
14. Rock and Roll — Velvet Underground
15. First We Take Manhattan — Leonard Cohen
16. Yeah! New York — Yeah Yeah Yeahs
17. Downtown Train — Tom Waits
18. The Scene — Atomic Number 76
19. Scrapple from the Apple — Charlie Parker
20. Harlem Shuffle — Bob and Earl
21. On Broadway — Drifters
22. New York New York — Dictators
23. I Am I Said — Neil Diamond
24. New York Skyline — Garland Jeffreys
25. Lower East Side — UK Subs
26. NYC Ghosts and Flowers — Sonic Youth
27. Crosstown Traffic — Jimi Hendrix
28. Slum Goddess of the Lower East Side — Fugs
29. Made in NYC — Casualties
30. New York New York — Frank Sinatra/Sid Vicious
31. Take the "A" Train — Duke Ellington
32. Olympia — Rancid
33. Going to New York — Jimmy Reed
34. Holiday Cocktail Lounge — Bouncing Souls
35. Subway Train — New York Dolls
36. New York City — John Lennon
37. Max's Kansas City — Jayne County and the Backstreet Boy
38. NYC 1999 — Pussy Galore
39. Holiday in Harlem — Ella Fitzgerald
40. New York City Serenade — Bruce Springsteen
41. Safe in New York City — AC/DC
42. Walk On the Wild Side — Lou Reed
43. Rockaway Beach — Ramones
44. Heartbreaker — Rolling Stones
45. I'm Waiting for the Man — Velvet Underground
46. Naked City — Kiss
47. Down and Out in New York City — James Brown
48. New York City — T. Rex
49. Hot in the City — Billy Idol
50. Funky Broadway — Wilson Pickett

51. Life During Wartime	Talking Heads	
52. New York 1963/America 1968	Animals	
53. NYC is Dead	L.E.S. Stitches	
54. Brooklyn Bound	Black Keys	
55. Coney Island Baby	Lou Reed	
56. A Letter to the New York Post	Public Enemy	
57. New York Was Great	Ravonettes	
58. New York Nights	Jesse Malin	
59. Cabbies On Crack	Ramones	
60. Egg Cream	Lou Reed	
61. All the Critics Love You in New York	Prince	
62. Positively 4th Street	Bob Dylan	
63. The Rising	Bruce Springsteen	
64. Union Square	Tom Waits	
65. Back to the Bronx	2 Live Crew	
66. Brooklyn Boogie	Louis Prima	
67. The Chelsea Hotel Oral Sex Song	Jeffery Lewis	
68. Brooklyn's Finest	Jay Z w/Notorious B.I.G.	
69. Chelsea Girls	Velvet Underground	
70. The Girl from New York City	Beach Boys	
71. Heartbreaker	Rolling Stones	
72. Incident on 57th Street	Bruce Springsteen	
73. Lightning Strikes	Clash	
74. Jamaican in New York	Shinehead	
75. Living For the City	Stevie Wonder	
76. Miss You	Rolling Stones	
77. Big Apple Dreamin'	Alice Cooper	
78. New York's in Love	David Bowie	
79. NYC Tonight	GG Allin	
80. Summer In the City	Lovin' Spoonful	
81. Tenth Avenue Freeze-Out	Bruce Springsteen	
82. Wimpy Drives Through Harlem	Queers	
83. Bronx	Kurtis Blow	
84. Sheena is a Punk Rocker	Ramones	
85. Times Square	Marianne Faithful	
86. Dirty Boulevard	Lou Reed	
87. Empire State Express	Son House	
88. Hard Times Iin New York	Bob Dylan	
89. I'm In the Mood	Elvis Costello	
90. New Killer Star	David Bowie	
91. New York	U2	
92. New York's My Home	Sammy Davis, Jr.	
93. We're a Happy Family	Ramones	
94. Whizz Kid	Mott The Hoople	
95. You Said Something	PJ Harvey	
96. N.Y. Stars	Lou Reed	
97. Chelsea Hotel No 2	Leonard Cohen	
98. Bleecker Street	Simon and Garfunkel	
99. Big Man On Mulberry Street	Billy Joel	
100. New York New York	Grandmaster Flash & The Furious Five	
101. Here Come the Yankees	Bundin/Stallman	

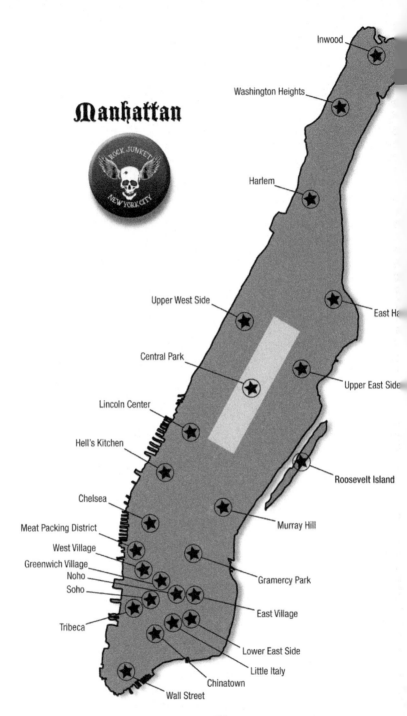

Manhattan

Inwood

Washington Heights

Harlem

Upper West Side

East Ha

Central Park

Upper East Side

Lincoln Center

Hell's Kitchen

Roosevelt Island

Chelsea

Meat Packing District

Murray Hill

West Village

Greenwich Village

Noho

Soho

Gramercy Park

Tribeca

East Village

Lower East Side

Little Italy

Chinatown

Wall Street

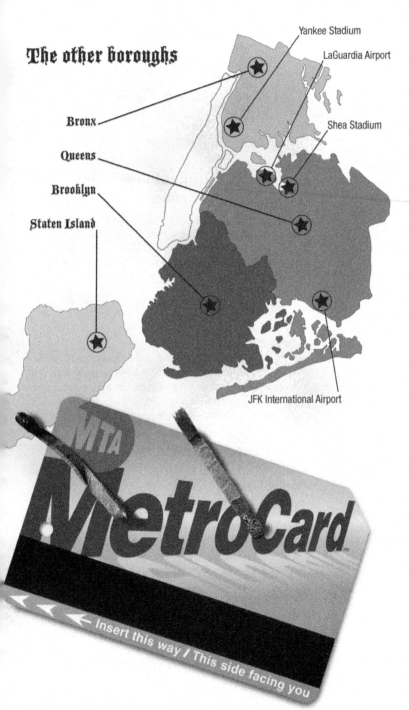

The other boroughs

- Yankee Stadium
- LaGuardia Airport
- Shea Stadium
- Bronx
- Queens
- Brooklyn
- Staten Island
- JFK International Airport

MTA MetroCard

← Insert this way / This side facing you

𝔚𝔞𝔩𝔨𝔦𝔫𝔤 𝔗𝔬𝔲𝔯𝔰
𝔉𝔞𝔫 𝔐𝔢𝔳𝔦𝔢𝔴𝔰

The catalyst for creating Rock Junket came from my
passion about music and the love of New York City.
This book is a natural extension of that foundation.
I wanted to share with you what Rock Junket fans are saying.
Below are a few unedited reviews fans were inspired to send me:

"Best part of our trip"

My fourteen year old and his friend are musicians and are serious music fans.
They loved the tour and were impressed with all of the knowledge and passion
for music that Bobby Pinn had. It was fun and interactive and two hours went by
so fast! They can't wait to go back and take a different tour. When I asked them
what was the best part of their NYC trip they said, "the rock tour"!

FrancineS, Female, Age range: 40–49
Domestic Tourist(s)—Family with Children
Wednesday, April 15th, 1:00 pm

"Amazing tour"

Bobby Pinn provides an excellent walking tour. His knowledge of music and
bands of the East Village is amazing. We loved how he talked about the bands
and individuals, provided picutres of the time, and also provided some trivia for
the group. The length of the tour was perfect and the pace was just right. I have
been recommending this tour to everyone we tell about our trip. Definitely worth
every penny!!!! Great fun!

meggers1972, Female, Age range: 30–39
International Tourist(s)—Family without Children
Saturday, February 14th, 11:00 am

"If you do ONE thing in NYC, make sure it's this!!!"

I am not gonna list all sites visited etc on this tour as previous excellent reviews already have! What I am going to stress to you though is, you simply must check this tour out!! Everything I know and love about music stems from this area! The bands, their lifestyle, their music and their influence on us even to this day! What Bobby does is bring to life amazing stories about these bands, their lifestyles, where they played, drank, shot their album cover etc. Chuck in some other East Village stories (including the ones you never got to hear about!!!) And what you have is a thrilling two hours! He speaks with such knowledge, passion and his natural enthusiasm for this subject is clear to see! Backed up with fantastic visuals and some classic insight, it was enough to make you feel like you lived the experiences right there in the village! Bobby we cannot thank you enough for such a great afternoon, it was definitely one of our best days whilst in NYC! Legend! Julie, Jake & Heather.

> juliepurple0, Female, Age range: 40–49
> International Tourist(s)—Family with Children
> Wednesday, July 16th, 1:00 pm

"Bobby Pinn is a ROCK STAR!"

Hands Down, best two hours spent in the city of the entire weekend!!! Bobby's knowledge and manner as a tour guide are beyond great! Would recommend this tour to any and all rock fans for the variety/quality of the information given on the tour! It's hard to pick a favorite part, loved the Led Zeppelin "Physical Graffitti" building, Trash & Vaudeville Store, Iggy Pop's condo......and on, and on! He is limitless in his knowledge and has such a warm/smooth presentation....makes you want more, more, more!!!!!

> jejrcook64, Female, Age range: 40-49
> Domestic Tourist(s)—Group of Friends
> Friday, October 17th, 1:00 pm

"Exciting fun-time tour extravaganza!"

This tour was perfect in every way. 1.-There were about 8 people total in the group, so the experience was personalized and engaging. 2.- Bobby knows all things, and was able to share information that even my extremely well read punk rocker of a boyfriend learned a few things. 3. Bobby knows all people, and it was cool when random characters walked up to say hello to him. Overall, it was a ve informative and entertaining tour, and i didn't feel like an "annoying tourist" in the small group. Bobby was very enthusiastic and fun, and it was obvious he loved his job. Having lived and travelled all over Europe, this was easily one of the best tours I have ever been on. Well worth the money.

One of the highlights of our trip.

> LeAnn84, Female, Age range: 20–29
> Domestic Tourist(s)—Couple on a Date
> Friday, December 12th, 1:00 pm

"One of the highlights of our trip"

Having been a fan of the various NYC punk bands from this area it was fantastic to get a nostalgic trip round the places I had only read about up to this point. I brought along my 13 year old daughter and apart from that the fact she had to walk was engrossed by Bobby's stories. Bobby was a fantastic tour guide, providing his own insight and experiences aided by a few props he brought along in his magic punk bag. I was supposed to do this tour on the Thu, but Bobby got in touch and offered me an alternative as the weather was supposed to be bad on that day (it did pour down on the Thu), but the Fri the weather was brilliant and it shows the effort Bobby puts in to make sure his tour is a success. We even back-tracked after the tour and took advantage of the discounts Bobby mentioned at one of the stores we passed during the tour and to try an egg-cream. I only have the highest praise for this tour and next time I am in NYC I hope to do the new tour Bobby mentioned, the Rock N Roll Pub Crawl.

> swpotter, Male, age range: 40–49
> International Tourist(s)—Family with Children
> Thursday, December 11th, 1:00 pm

highly recommend this awesome musical odyssey"

My girlfriend and I did the Rock & Punk tour last weekend. Probably the best 2 hours of our NYC trip. If you love music, this is the tour for you!!!

> mcbrown76, Male, Age range: 30–39
> Domestic Tourist(s)—Couple on a Date
> Friday, November 7th, 1:00 pm

Great fun and very informative"

Some great stories from a guide who makes the area come to life and gives you a better sense of its past. Ours was a really diverse group of people, but all seemed to have a great time.. My partner was only along with me out of duty - he has no interest in music !! Even he was captivated by the stories and ended up enjoying the tour, despite his reservations! I loved every minute of it.

Enlightening, exhilarating, totally rock 'n' roll!

> jaynebrown, Female, Age range: 50–59
> International Tourist(s)—Other
> Saturday, September 27th, 11:00 am

'Enlightening, exhilarating, totally rock n' roll!"

Bobby Pinn is a spiky haired, animated, friendly and thoroughly knowledgeable guide. He is well suited to conducting this tour as he looks like a rock star himself. I took my 18 year-old daughter on the tour in August 2008 and we both enjoyed it despite the fact that she hadn't heard of a lot of the bands and artists. If you are into punk rock especially I would heartily recommend it. Bobby is very thorough and entertaining in his delivery and invites questions so don't hold back. There are many bars and eateries en route, some of which Bobby recommends. We particularly liked the fashion shops and at the end of the tour I would urge anyone to visit Trash and Vaudeville which is at the beginning of the route. The tour ends at the former CBGBs, now a gallery, and that's also worth a look. The staff in there are also very helpful and friendly. One piece of advice though: the tour is 2 hours long and we went in sweltering heat, so wear comfortable clothes and shoes.

> 80schick, Female, Age range: 40–49
> International Tourist(s)—Family with Children
> Friday, August 29th, 1:00 pm

"Bobby Pinn is a true Rock N Roll Historian!"

As a native New Yorker and Rock N Roll lover I thought I knew everything there was to know about Rock n Roll history til I took this tour with Bobby Pinn. This guy is amazing!

> AVYBETH, Female, Age range: 50–59
> Local—Group of Friends
> Saturday, August 23rd,11:00 am

"A Big Apple highlight"

We brought our kids from London to NYC for the first time - there's so much to wow them but this was a definate top trump with us and them. Bobby's tour of the East Viallage was perfectly pitched for all and brimming with anecdotes, insights and heritage. Unreservedly recommended for music fans of all ages.

> gricefamily, Male, Age range: 40–49
> International Tourist(s)—Family with Children
> Saturday, July 26th, 11:00 am

"A Brilliant Tour"

I have to say this is the best thing we did in New York. I love the Ramones and punk rock music from the 70's and 80's and really enjoyed the afternoon My girlfriend is into Celine Dion and she loved the tour as well! (She loved the stories and it has now given her a taste for the music). If you have any interest in what was going on in the New York scene or just love your music then this is the tour for you!

> roblucas, Male, Age range: 30–39
> International Tourist(s)—Individual
> Wednesday, August 6th, 1:00 pm

"awesome"

the tour was really unique and not the typical tours that are out there that take you to the common tourist attractions we all know already....all the explanations were great and it was really cool to learn about who and what had to do with the buildings we walk by...it was an awesome tour...i wish there were more like this!

> sandramv3, Female, Age range: 30–39
> Domestic Tourist(s)—Individual
> Thusday, August 7th, 1:00 pm

"So Great"

The stories were amazing and there was so much detail. One of the best tours I have ever been on.

> bbdayley, Male, Age range: 20–29
> Domestic Tourist(s)—Family without Children
> Wednesday, July 16th, 1:00 pm

And we thought we knew all about punk rock!"

I am 45 years old my daughter is 18. We are both fans of punk rock because I lived in the era and my daughter just thinks it's really cool. She went into the tour knowing a lot more than me about the bands, venues, etc. However, we both learned so much! It was so interesting and fun. It was certainly not touristy and not sugar coated. If you're a true punk rock fan, this is the tour for you. Trust me, you may think you know it all....but you will learn a lot. Bobby Pinn was the best tour guide ever. And....he'll take you to a pub after if you'd like to keep talking. I would not, however reccomend this tour if you are looking for the little old lady historical tour. It gets a little graphic, but it's real and we LOVED it!

> TERESALONG, Female, Age range: 40–49
> Domestic Tourist(s)—Other
> Saturday, July 5th, 11:00 am

It f***in rocked!"

Bobby Pinn knows his stuff. By being part of the music industry, he obviously gained knowledge and experience in the field. He resides in NY - the rock and roll center of the country. The tour was everything I thought it would be and more. If you are ever in NY, make sure you check this out. Keep on rockin in the free world!

> NancyDavis, Male, Age range: Under 20
> Domestic Tourist(s)—Family with Children
> Friday, July 25th, 1:00 pm

Lots of walk, talk, and rock"

We had a great time on Bobby Pinn's East Village Rock Junket tour - which included the Joe Strummer "The Future is Unwritten" mural, Charlie Parker's home, Joey Ramone's former apartment, Madonna's former apartment, and the the former sites of CBGBs and the Filmore. As Canadians from the province of Manitoba, it was a special delight to see Handsome Dick Manitoba's bar in the East Village (called "Manitoba's"). Bobby knows his music and loves to talk; he'll remind you of the punk older brother you had who always had more records and knew more about them than you. His knowledge and taste are impeccable, and he even made me believe that I should give Iggy's Avenue B album another listen. Wow! At the end of the tour, Bobby gives you a brochure with "things to do" recommendations, including having an egg cream from the Gem (on Second Avenue at St. Mark's Place) and riding the Cyclone at Coney Island, which turned out to be two other big highlights of our trip. We went on the tour on a very hot day. If you do, bring some water and even a snack, so you can stand for two hours without falling over. Looking forward to taking another one of Bobby's tours on the next trip. - Kenton and Caroline, Winnipeg, Canada

> kentonlarsen, Male, Age range: 40–49
> International Tourist(s)—Other
> Wednesday, July 16th, 1:00 pm

Bobby Pinn, a.k.a. Ron Colinear, was born in Pittsburgh, Pennsylvania, and has been a fan of music since he bought his first single "Satisfaction" by the Rolling Stones.

Ron moved to New York City in 1990 and began a 17-year career as an executive in the music business, before founding Rock Junket, a multi-tiered rock tourism and entertainment empire. He lives in Manhattan and remains a fan of music, art, fashion, New York City, the Pittsburgh Steelers, and he still loves the Stones.

You'll be able to find him nowadays hosting his walking tours, working on his TV concept, creating pop culture board games, writing another book, **About the Author** getting more tattoos, visiting art museums, checking out rock shows, golfing in Brooklyn, having a Guinness at one of his favorite pubs or sitting in Yankee Stadium cheering on his beloved Yanks.

And when in New York, take his tours, have a beer with him and enjoy the rich musical history of New York City that he shares so eloquently.

Thanks

After I finished writing this book, I asked myself whom should I thank?
Let's start with the bands, artists, musicians, writers,
painters and photographers who have influenced my life
and this book.

Without them I probably would not have moved to
New York, and this city would have missed out on
a very creative era that they helped mold. But I also
need to thank some friends and colleagues who
believed in my many visions.

They are Larry Germack (my oldest and
dearest friend and a true genius), Billy The
Artist (a great friend, visionary and my
favorite artist), Darlene Samer, Sam Nole,
Bingo Sanatra, Jill Hopler, Greg Wood,
Duncan Hutchinson, Eric Tremblay, Edith
Bellinghausen, Dan Levine, Rob Chapman,
Dalton Ross, Roland Grybauskus, Lisa
Larson, Brett Green, Mark Kraynak, Mike
Kraynak, Johnny "The Chief" Colinear, Sue
Frost, Jimmy Webb, Craig Collins, Todd
Baker, Wilma Garcia, Shaun Clancy, Suke
Yawata, Mary Dunston, Ross Stoner, Gmac,
Roberta Baley, Mike Del Tufo, Vinnie at
Generation Records, Rob Partington, Karen
Disher, Juilliard and The Mid-Manhattan
Library, Warren Schatz, Wyno and Helen
at Morrison Hotel Gallery, Barry Koven,
my friends and bartenders at Bull McCabe's
Foley's, Desmond's Tavern, Swift and
International Bar, Mary, Linda and Jim,
and my brothers and sister John, Bill
and Joann.

But most of all, to paraphrase Dee Dee Ramone
during his Hall of Fame induction speech, I would like
to thank myself and give myself a big fucking pat on
the back.

Also a big rock n' roll thank you to Lisa Larson who had the energy, creativity
and vision to design this book. Visit Lisa's site at www.lisa-larson.com.
All content and pictures by Bobby Pinn Rock Junket. Edited by Larry Germack.

To my mom Ann and my dad John,
who both passed away in 2007.

Rock Junket, LLC, is a multi-tiered entertainment business based in New York City.

Bobby Pinn's walking tours have been covered by *The New York Times*, *Daily News*, *New York Post*, *New York Magazine*, *Entertainment Weekly*, *Rolling Stone*, *The Villager*, *Billboard*, *Washington Post*, *Guardian U.K.*, *The Telegraph U.K.*, *Melbourne Herald Sun*, *Artindustry U.K.*, *Time Out New York and Reforma De Viaje*, Mexico.

Bobby Pinn has also been featured on television shows in Germany, Sweden, England, United States, Mexico, South America and Italy.

Visit your iPhone App store to download Rock Junket Tour apps and games.

Join our mailing list for periodical updates regarding the New York music scene and become a friend of ours on Facebook.

If you would like to book a tour, buy merchandise or to tell us what you thought of the book visit www.rockjunket.com.

CPSIA information can be obtained
at www.ICGtesting.com
Printed in the USA
BVOW06s2023100217
475922BV00006B/21/P